Quilting Bees

SWARMS OF IDEAS AND PROJECTS TO SHARE

BY BARBARA TONE LISTER & SHERRI BAIN DRIVER

To a quilt group this question was posed,
"When I'm old can I still quilt—who knows!?"
Then came the reply,
"Old quilters don't die,
They just become old sew 'n sews!"

by Donna Driver

POSSIBILITIES®

8970 E. HAMPDEN AVE. DENVER, CO 80231
PHONE 303-740-6206   FAX 303-220-7424

▼ DEDICATION ▼

We dedicate our book to Gary, Holly, and Garrett Lister, and
Rob, Ryan, and Reanna Driver. Thanks for BEE-lieving in us.

▼ ACKNOWLEDGEMENTS ▼

We would like to thank all the bees that helped us with our research:
Over the Edge Quilters, Bethany Lutheran Church Quilters, The Wednesday Bee, Never Say Die Quilters, The Parker Bag Ladies, Tuesday Nite Bee, Patchworkers, On-Line Quilters: Chapter II, Quilt Explorations, Piecemakers, Great American Quilters, Homestead Friendship Sampler Quilt Bee, M&Ms, Mother's Day Quilters, Thursday Night Therapy (TNT), THE Quilt Group, Patch Workers, Interfaith Quilters, Haole Connection, Art Quiltists, Aurora Piecemakers, Afternoon Delight, St. Vrain Valley Quilters, SEA-Q, Moms, Coral Gables Congregation Church Bee.

We would like to give special thanks to the following individuals:

Nancy Smith, Lynda Milligan, Sharon Holmes, Marilyn Robinson, Susan Dumler,
and Jane Dumler for their valuable suggestions and constant encouragement.

Gary Lister for his photographic expertise and wonderful cents of humor (about 2¢ worth).

Chris Brown, Mary Beth Church, Judy Kraus, Leslie Lott, Carol Medsker, Janet Robinson, Sandy Sanford,
Alison Schwabe, and Janet Jo Smith (the members of our quilting bee) for never saying "no" to us.

Rosemary Angelos, Joan Campbell, Helen Davis, Marilyn Dillard, Linda Dixon, Viola Flowers, Brenda Groelz, Rusty Miller, Jan Rold, Christine Scott, Jean Shepperly, Phyllis Solakian, Betty Thompson, Shirley Wegert, Sandy Wheeler, and Carol Wiegal for being so generous with their time and sharing information about their bees.

Donna Cook, Emmy Midkiff, and Ann Sturm for sharing their charts.

Holly and Garrett Lister, Thomas Peter Johnson, and Ryan and Reanna Driver for their baking skills.

Donna Driver for her silly poetry.

Dan Trujillo for being there when we needed him.

The staff at Possibilities and Great American Quilt Factory for their patience and constant enthusiasm.

The women who graciously allowed us to feature their quilts.

▼ CREDITS ▼

Executive Editors – Nancy Smith and Lynda Milligan
Senior Editor – Sharon Holmes
Design & Illustration – Marilyn Robinson
Electronic Illustration – Sharon Holmes
Photography – Brian Birlauf

Table of Contents

Introduction

Membership in quilting bees has brought us countless hours of pleasure and priceless friendships. As an added bonus we have many beautiful quilts that have been made as bee projects. We are both members of a bee that started in 1987. At that time one of us had already been quilting for eight years and the other was a BEE-ginner.

Showing our group quilts at local guild meetings, we were swamped with questions about bees. What does a bee do? How can I find one? How can I start a bee? How can a bee organize group projects? We realized that during our years in bees we made numerous projects and had stored up a great deal of knowledge about how a bee works. Our lives

have truly been enriched by our involvement in quilting bees, and we want to share what we have learned and encourage women to join a bee or to form new groups.

We knew about our own bee but thought we should find out about other groups so we could offer a wide range of ideas. And so the interviews began... There were groups we had already heard of through friends and family, and others were brought to our attention when people learned that we were gathering information for a book. We met many warm and gracious women who invited us into their homes and meeting places to share their experiences with quilting bees.

WHAT IS A QUILTING BEE?

A dictionary defines "bee" as a community social gathering to perform some task. Another definition refers to being obsessed with one idea or having eccentric and fanciful ideas, like a bee in her bonnet. We think these are both descriptive of the quilting groups we have visited. Bees are certainly social gatherings caught up in the excitement of producing beautiful and fanciful quilts, and many members are truly obsessed with quilt making. For the purpose of this book, we think of a bee as a small and relatively informal gathering of friends doing anything

associated with quilts. There are groups that are strictly social, some meet to make quilts to donate to charity, and others gather to learn about the art or craft of quilt making.

During our research we met some women who objected to the word "bee". We tried to think of a better term and came up with "network", but the word seemed too trendy and awkward. We finally decided that "bee" is simply a buzz-word for network, and that is what we have used for this book.

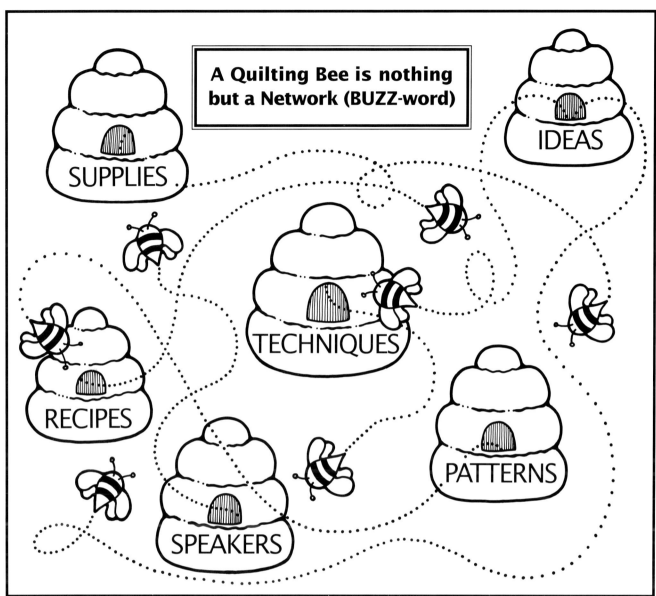

A Quilting Bee is nothing but a Network (BUZZ-word)

SUPPLIES

IDEAS

TECHNIQUES

RECIPES

PATTERNS

SPEAKERS

 **WHY BEE-LONG?**

Membership in a bee offers many benefits. Meetings are perfect opportunities to learn new quilting skills as members share knowledge of techniques as well as books, patterns, and new products. On the surface quilting seems like the main purpose of a bee, but sewing is often secondary to the friendships made in the group.

A friend who has moved frequently says that she no longer spends her time trying to make

friends with nonquilters. They can not understand anyone who collects yards and yards of fabric, cuts it into small pieces, and then sews it all back together. She concentrates instead on meeting other quilters and finds instant rapport every time she moves into a new community. Women have mentioned how important it is to find a connection with other women, and many of them have found a special niche in quilting bees.

As a guest on The Oprah Winfrey Show, Gloria Steinem spoke about self-esteem. When a woman asked how to build self-esteem when it is at a low point, Gloria answered, "Find a couple of friends and make a kind of alternate family that meets once a week. It doesn't matter what you call it, quilting bee, lunching club, CR group—doesn't matter—but people who love you and care about you. Just make sure you meet with them every week."

Most people need to feel they belong to some kind of group and are a part of something grander than themselves. Bee membership can give a sense of community—women held together by a common interest in quilting. Members can attend events together such as guild meetings, quilt shows, and classes. Quilting bees can become involved in making charitable projects and give a part of themselves back to the community.

Showing a circle of friends a finished quilt or one in progress brings out real appreciation and enthusiasm. This kind of encouragement is important to all of us and can be hard to find among people who do not understand the amount of work that goes into making a quilt. Magic happens over a quilting frame or in a sewing circle—women stitch together deep and lasting friendships.

BEE-coming a Member

Once you have decided to join a bee, some investigative work may be required to find a bee with openings for new members. It is also possible to start a new bee and have a part in planning its traditions and activities. The following information will guide the way.

FINDING AN EXISTING BEE

One of the first places to look for a bee with openings is the local quilt guild. Many guilds encourage bee membership as a way for members to become better acquainted in small group settings. Guilds may have a "beekeeper" volunteer who coordinates setting up new bees, placing members in existing bees, and posting articles on the subject in the newsletter. Quarterly coffees or meetings can be arranged by the beekeeper to describe the activities of bees and gather women who are interested in joining. At the meeting members can compare their quilting skills and plan a bee meeting time that is agreeable to the majority. The guild's newsletter may feature a list of groups with openings or individuals interested in joining a group.

For areas without a quilt guild, the following groups or individuals may sponsor or know of quilting bees with possible openings.
- Embroidery or sewing guilds
- Quilt or fabric shops—ask shop owner or check for flyers or bulletin board notices
- Neighborhood, church, recreation center, and newcomer groups
- Fellow students in quilting classes or workshops

Questions to Ask

Once you have found a bee, asking some questions prior to attending a meeting will help you decide if the group has goals similar to yours.

- Are the members beginners, advanced, or a mix of abilities?
- Does the group work together at a frame or work on individual projects?
- Are group projects such as exchanges or rotations planned and how often?
- Are the members' ages diverse or clustered?
- Is the group focused on one style or aspect of quilting such as a specialty bee?

 # STARTING A NEW BEE

Forming a new bee may sound a bit scary and hard, but really it is not. Since the group is new, the meeting time and day, make-up of the members, and organizational ideas may all be tailored to your desires. Even the meeting location is open to selection. Once these details are decided, the next step is extending invitations to prospective members for the first meeting.

When and Where to Meet

Any meeting time can be chosen to fit your needs. Groups can meet in the evening or during the day. Day groups can be arranged for morning, afternoon, or all-day sessions. Some groups plan a beginning and ending time with members arriving and departing anytime within that framework, for example 9 a.m. to 3 p.m. Bees can be scheduled for any day of the week. Saturday may work beautifully for working women.

Groups working on charitable projects requiring set-up time may wish to meet on two consecutive days every other week. A group with mothers of young children may wish to suspend meeting during the summer months except for a few special outings.

Meetings can be held in churches, libraries, recreation centers, and quilt shop classrooms. However, most bees meet in members' homes for a more intimate setting. The meetings can rotate among the members on a random schedule that is decided a few weeks to a month ahead, or a yearly schedule can be planned. Some groups have a hostess of the month, and the meetings occur at her home during that time. Just think, eleven months before you need to clean your house for quilt group!

Advertising for Members

If there are still openings in the bee after inviting your friends, an ad placed in area newsletters or on bulletin boards may generate additional interest. Also, the local quilt shop may be very happy to place an ad in their class newsletter. The following notices were placed in a quilt guild's newsletter and resulted in the addition of several new members.

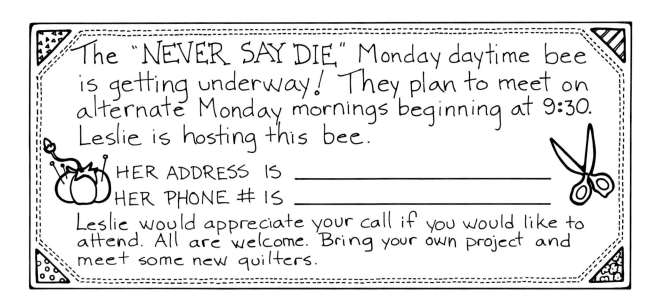

The "NEVER SAY DIE" Monday daytime bee is getting underway! They plan to meet on alternate Monday mornings beginning at 9:30. Leslie is hosting this bee.

HER ADDRESS IS _____

HER PHONE # IS _____

Leslie would appreciate your call if you would like to attend. All are welcome. Bring your own project and meet some new quilters.

O Christmas Bee, O Christmas Bee How Lovely Are Thy Projects!

Dig out those unfinished projects, Christmas dream quilts, and new patterns you've been collecting and join Arapahoe County Quilters' new Christmas Bee! What better way to get new ornaments on the tree or quilts on the beds than to set aside the first Monday of the month from 9:30 a.m. until 1:00, 2:00, or 3:00 p.m.

If this idea suits your Christmas fancy, call Sandra at

_____.

Meetings will be at Great American.

First Meeting

At the first meeting members can discuss activities that they would like to try and how they envision the bee. Each person might tell about her quilting background and show some quilts. Time can be devoted to discussing guidelines for the group, if any, and planning the schedule for the next few meetings.

Bee Government

Few rules, no elected officers, and an open agenda make bee membership a pleasant experience. Once a bee decides when and where to meet, the activities can be free-flowing with just enough organization so everyone knows when things are happening. Incorporating some of the following organizational ideas may help the bee buzz smoothly along.

 LEADER OF THE HIVE — "QUEEN BEE"

Many bees function without an appointed leader. If a member proposes an idea or activity that the others wish to undertake, it is understood that the instigator will oversee any details or deadlines involved with the project. At any time two or three ladies may be leading a variety of projects. Sometimes the leader may need to provide written directions to clarify information about the activity such as yardage, order of events, and due dates. At other times, once an idea is embraced, the group may need no guidance.

Another approach is to have members suggest ideas for the group and then have someone volunteer to be in charge of the chosen project. Many groups report that this is a time when you do not want to leave the room. During your absence you may be appointed to be leader of the pack, and the group may have decided on a BEE-hemoth project!

Some groups may feel more comfortable appointing one member to serve as the "queen bee". Rotating this position every six months will keep the time of leadership short and allow each member a chance to guide the bee. Some groups provide the "queen bee" with a bell that she can ring to get everyone's attention for group votes.

Appointing a member to serve as secretary to record or publish notes about meetings is unnecessary. If a member is absent, she can catch up at the next meeting or call another member to ask what she missed.

ROSTER

It is very helpful to have a roster listing each member's name, address, phone number, and perhaps birth date. As members are added and deleted from the group, an updated version may be necessary. Often, one member will volunteer to type the list when the need arises.

The roster is the perfect place to record the names of children, spouses, and interesting information as it is revealed. Special dietary likes and dislikes can also be recorded to help plan refreshments.

DUES

Generally, dues are not necessary for a bee. Incidental expenses may be incurred for greeting cards, flowers, gifts sent by the group, or entry fees for a contest. Collecting an equal amount from each member when the need arises can handle these infrequent costs. For some groups, it may be easier to have a small "kitty" for occasional expenses, with each member contributing five to ten dollars at the beginning of each year. The bee may decide that expenses up to a certain limit may be incurred without group approval. Anything beyond that amount will require discussion and a group vote. Bees that contribute regularly to charitable causes or exhibit their quilts may need to have yearly dues to cover these ongoing expenses.

SCHEDULING MEETINGS

An easy and quick way to schedule meeting locations and outings is to periodically whip out calendars and plan for the next two or three months. If each member volunteers to host a meeting at some time during the three months, the location rotation will generally be evenly distributed. Planning in this way usually requires few schedule changes, as members will often know of vacations, school holidays, and special commitments a few months in advance.

Some groups prefer to make a yearly calendar that includes traditional luncheons, and they assign hostesses in a predetermined order. This plan does not allow flexibility for attending activities not planned a year in advance. The roster and yearly schedule can be combined and handed out at the beginning of the year.

Meeting for an entire month at one member's home may be perfect for a group that quilts at a frame. Entertaining duties will be completed in one month, and the meetings will rotate among all the members before returning to your home. Carefully scheduling all entertaining obligations during the month you serve as hostess will immensely diminish chores—more quilting time!

ADDING NEW MEMBERS

A few discussions will determine how your bee wishes to add new members. Including new members can be richly rewarding, infusing the group with new ideas and personalities, or an unfortunate choice may upset the balance of a cohesive group. The following ideas might be considered prior to inviting a new member.

- Open membership to anyone who is interested in joining.
- Groups may prefer to select a member they feel will fit in the bee. If an opening occurs, members may suggest friends or quilters they know as potential members. If no objections are raised, an invitation can be extended. One member can volunteer to explain the group's activities and accompany the new member to her first bee.
- Some groups decide not to add new members. They enjoy the bee just as it is and do not wish to upset the closeness the group has developed. Bees that have met for a number of years develop a history together, which may make it difficult for a new member to feel included.

PROPER BEE-HAVIOR

Adopting a few bee etiquette guidelines will keep a bee buzzing along with few problems. Members normally view bee time as a relaxing treat. The following are for your group's consideration.

- Be prompt.
- Let the hostess know if you will be late or absent.
- Try to spend more time listening than talking.
- Include everyone in the conversation.
- Be positive and offer encouragement.
- When extending invitations for outings or discussing other groups that you may belong to, be sure to invite everyone at the bee or make your arrangements at another time. It hurts to feel excluded.
- Avoid stinging gossip.
- Consider changing the subject if the discussion becomes heated and disagreeable. Controversial subjects such as religion, politics, and sex may need to be avoided if opinions are too strong.
- Leave at the designated time. The hostess may have to hit the road for other commitments.

ARISTOTLE ONCE SAID, "WE SHOULD BEHAVE TO OUR FRIENDS AS WE WOULD WISH OUR FRIENDS TO BEHAVE TO US."

What Does a Bee Do-Bee-Do?

Members of quilting bees obviously spend a great deal of time sewing, but they engage in other activities, too. As friendships grow, the activities enjoyed by the group may expand and make the bonds even stronger. The following ideas may tempt your group.

SHARING

Bee members often share information about a variety of subjects related to quilting. This happens in nearly every bee in an informal manner as one member asks another for advice on a particular project. A bee might benefit from sharing in a more organized way. Members can teach each other tried-and-true quilting methods as well as new techniques learned from books and classes. Members might take turns teaching or demonstrating on a monthly or weekly basis. There are always new books and tools on the market and new classes being taught, so there should be a never-ending list of topics to share.

A bee might want to devote a larger amount of time to learning about some phase of quilt making. Some quilt shops rent instructional videos, and a bee might choose to view these together. Computer programs for designing quilts might be an interesting subject for a bee to explore. A group can use bee meeting time to study a book about a particular aspect of quilt making such as color theory. There are several books on the market that include lessons and exercises in such aspects of quilt making as machine piecing or surface embellishment. Members can do weekly homework assignments as described in the book and share their results with the other members. It might be helpful to have one member organize the lessons by breaking them into small segments.

A group interested in buying new sewing machines might investigate each brand's features and discuss them. Stores often give discounts if several machines are purchased at the same time, and if a class is offered for new machine owners, the bee can enjoy learning together.

Sharing does not need to be limited to sewing. Members can share information about shows to view, contests to enter, or photos of out-of-town quilt exhibits. Some groups trade recipes and novels. One bee shares books on tape that can be enjoyed while sewing.

HELPING

Bee members can get together to help with the less exciting phases of quilt making. Basting quilts can be a tedious job, but when friends help the work goes fast, and it can actually be fun. A special day can be set aside for basting. Each member with a project to layer needs to bring all the supplies for her own quilt—top, batting, backing, and safety pins or needles and thread. Some shops encourage customers to use large classroom tables for basting when there are no classes scheduled.

Many quilters believe that binding is the worst part of quilt making. This is another task that can be done together. If a quilt is very large, one bee member can work on each side. Just BEE-ware that you will be expected to reciprocate.

Quilt shows and historical museums sometimes ask groups to demonstrate needlework skills to the public. A bee may volunteer to quilt on a frame or dress in period costumes.

A bee might be interested in volunteering to help individuals or groups outside their own bee. Members might like to make quilts to donate to a deserving organization. Suggestions for charitable activities can be found on pages 24 to 26. If bee members also belong to a guild, they might help with a raffle project or other committee within the guild. One bee has an understanding that if any bee member takes on a committee chair position in her guild, all the other members will help on the committee, but they are careful not to volunteer their friends too often.

Life is full of unexpected turns, and bee members often help friends through difficult times. Many women we interviewed said that bee members helped them through family illnesses, deaths, and divorces by providing emotional support as well as material items. One bee temporarily furnished a house for a friend who had lost her home in a hurricane.

ESTABLISHING GROUP IDENTITY

Creating a sense of closeness and camaraderie among bee members can be enhanced by adopting a group name, photographing and recording the quilts and activities of the group in scrapbooks, and having a bee "uniform".

The Name Game

Selecting just the right name for your bee may take some careful consideration and a democratic paper vote. The group's name can reflect when the group meets, its sense of humor, style of quilting, values, or place in the community. Through the years the group may explore new interests and evolve into a different type of group. Changing the group's name to reflect these new interests is certainly acceptable. Research for this book turned up some common names but also some very creative ones. The following list of names is a sampling of bee names we heard.

Never Say Die Quilters
Quilt Explorations
Piecemakers
Piece Corps
Homestead Friendship Sampler
Scrap Happy Quilters
Over the Edge Quilters
Material Girls
Gab and Giggle
Stitch 'n Bitch
Foxy Quilters
Friday Block Party
On-line Quilters (Computer Group)
Zombees (A Night Group)
Nimble Thimbles
Little House of Quilters
Patchin' Pals
Patchworkers
Parker Bag Ladies

Haole Connection
Happy Hoopers
Variable Star Quilters
Pine Needlers
Quilt Batts
Willing Workers of Atchinson
Fabriholics
Fabric Friends or is it Fiends
Friendship Circle
Patchin' Partners
Eight Hands Around
Never Enough Quilts
Ladies of the Evening
Hands All Around
Quilters From Heck
M&Ms—This group will not reveal the meaning of their name until you have joined and attended for awhile. They've met for twelve-plus years, and it's still a secret.

Saving Memories

A scrapbook filled with photos of members and activities will preserve the history of the bee. It's surprising how quickly time passes and how fast the details of the bee's activities can be forgotten.

As each member joins the group, her name and the date can be added to a cumulative roster. When she moves, returns to work, or needs to leave the group, the date can be noted. For a charitable group a similar list can record each completed quilt and for whom it was made. Adding a photo for each listing will also provide a visual record. A project that incurs some expenses (theme rotation quilt) or generates some revenue (quilting for a fee or making a raffle quilt) might be recorded for future reference.

The I Go to Pieces chart on the next page is an example of how one member records the exchanges she participates in. Each member's name is listed in one column, and the types of exchanges are named across the top. This serves as a handy way to note names of blocks received and given and to record historical information. One member's short

time of membership is noted by her participation in only one exchange. It might be helpful to include dates in your chart.

A member may wish to make a personal record of the group's exchanges by creating duplicate blocks for herself. A coordinated selection of fabrics can be set aside for the blocks, and after a number of years there will be enough to make a sampler. Each block will be a lovely and lasting reminder of one of the bee members.

 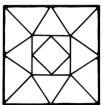

I GO TO PIECES
Blocks given and received by Ann Sturm

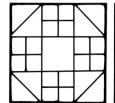 

Name	Heart Block Exchange	Christmas Block Exchange	Good-bye Blocks	Block of the Month	Block of the Month	Other Blocks Given	Blocks Received
Diane			Album red/white			ACQ Pres. - Colo. block	spool trade
Betty		girl block					
Barb	woven heart (pieced)		Four Corners Graffiti	Pinwheel block - red/blue/tan		ACQ Pres. - neon cats on black	New Mexico block
Janet	pieced heart			tree			Colorado block
Jerre	pieced heart	Card Trick	House in Heart	Country Cousin	Snowball		Mississippi block
Lucy	dolls & hearts appl.	teddy bear appliqué		Crown of Thorns	Storm at Sea		California block
Penny	mouse stencil in heart appl.	flower appliqué	little girl block	Dresden Plate	Peony (scrap)		Drunkard's Path pillow - Louisiana block
Lisa★	heart appliqué		Four Corners	baby heart			Michigan block

★The blocks Ann gave to Lisa were a heart appliqué block in the Heart Block Exchange, a Four Corners block as a Good-bye Block when she moved, and a baby heart block for Lisa's Block of the Month. From Lisa Ann received a Michigan block for her Block of the Month exchange.

Distinctive Duds

Many groups enjoy attending quilting events as a group, be it a seminar, quilt exhibit, guild meeting, or a day of group shopping. On these outing days it can be great fun to wear matching clothing or name tags.

The following items have been used for other groups and might stimulate some ideas for your bee.

- Patchwork shirts. Purchase ready-made denim shirts and have each member add lace, embroidery, and patchwork. Each shirt will be unique but similar enough to show that you BEE-long together.

16

- Baseball caps. Purchase similar caps and place the bee's logo and/or name on the caps or have each member add her own embellishments (rhinestones, puffy paint, Seminole piecing).
- Tote bags. Purchase a tote bag and apply the group's name. One group had a mini-class at the bee with members making identical bags. They enjoyed the totes so much, they changed their name to the Parker Bag Ladies.
- Vests. Select a vest pattern and background fabric. Use stenciling or embroidery to add the bee's name.
- Pins. Choose a uniform pin created from fabric or a metal one made at a sports trophy shop. One group selected a miniature doll to make at a bee meeting, and it became part of their logo.

- Tee-shirts. Transfer a silk-screen design or hand paint a plain tee-shirt to create a fun "uniform". It is also possible to purchase a tee-shirt featuring a quilt design and apply the bee's name to the back. A heat transfer from a group photo can also be used to decorate a tee.

Bee Booties

BEE-lieve it or not, one group reports that an elderly relative of one member loves to make crocheted booties in vast quantities. In an effort to rid her drawers of these slippers, the member convinced the others to wear them at bee meetings during the winter. Each year members are provided with a new pair. As yet, the bee has not been spotted in public wearing the "group uniform".

 # FOOD — HONEY FOR THE HIVE

It may seem strange to include a section about food in a quilt book, but most bees serve refreshments. One bee, determined to keep things simple, asks the hostess to provide a large pot of coffee, and that is all. If members want anything else, they need to bring it themselves. On the other extreme, some hostesses prepare gourmet meals and even set tables with their finest china and silver. A member who did not consider herself a very good cook was worried about what she would prepare when her turn came to host the bee for lunch. She prepared her favorite casserole, and the group gave her recipe the seal of approval. Now she confidently serves the same casserole every time the bee meets in her home. Another bee served elegant meals for a year, but after all the ladies' fancy dishes had been seen, the big meals were pared down so more time could be spent sewing. Most bees take the middle ground on refreshments, having the hostess provide beverages and a light snack. (Often, only chocolate is allowed!)

Pot luck meals can be arranged several times a year to celebrate special occasions or just BEE-cause it's fun. One group plans a potluck at Christmas and one other time during the year. (The second potluck is planned whenever members notice that they have not had one for awhile.) Carefully planning the luncheon can insure that at least half of the members bring dessert. A few nutritious items can be brought just to make the members feel healthy. ***Life is uncertain—eat dessert first!***

Here are a few of our favorite recipes:

Stinger

½ oz. white crème de menthe
1 oz. brandy

Shake with ice and strain into a chilled cocktail glass.

Fruit Salad by Committee

Each bee member brings one kind of cut-up fruit, and they are all combined in a large bowl. Pour Honey Fruit Dressing over the salad and enjoy!

Honey Fruit Dressing

Makes approximately 1½ cups

⅓ cup honey ⅓ cup sugar
1 t salt 1 t paprika
1 t mustard ¾ cup salad oil
1 t celery seed ¼ cup lemon juice

Shake well in a tightly covered jar and serve with fruit salad.

Honey Curry Spread

Makes approximately 1¼ cups

1 T minced onion
8 oz. cream cheese
2 T curry powder
2 t Worchestershire sauce
2 T honey
2 T fresh lemon juice
⅛ t cayenne pepper

Combine all ingredients well. Refrigerate, covered, at least two hours to combine flavors. Serve with crackers.

Honey Wheat Bread

*Makes two 9″ x 5″ loaves
(or 24 cloverleaf rolls)*

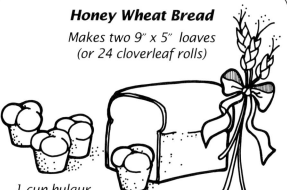

1 cup bulgur
3 T butter
1½ cups boiling water
1¼ cups cold water
2 t salt
½ cup honey
1 pkg. dry yeast
¾ cup warm water (105˚ to 115˚)
3 cups stone-ground whole wheat flour
2 to 3 cups unbleached flour

In large bowl, combine bulgur, butter, and boiling water. Let stand 30 minutes. Stir in cold water, salt, and honey. Combine yeast and warm water. Stir with fork and let stand 5 minutes. Add to bulgur mixture. Stir in whole wheat flour and enough unbleached flour to make a fairly stiff dough. Turn out on floured board and knead until smooth and elastic, or use mixer dough hook. Place dough in oiled bowl and turn to oil top. Cover and let rise until doubled, about 1½ hours. Punch down and shape into loaves (or rolls). Place in 2 greased 9″ x 5″ loaf pans (or in muffin tins). Cover and let rise until dough rises to tops of pans, about 45 minutes. Bake in preheated 375˚ oven 35 to 40 minutes or until bread is brown and loaves sound hollow when tapped on bottom. Cool on racks.

Scrap Soup

Makes approximately 3 quarts

1 lb. boned chicken breast
7-8 cups chicken broth
1 onion, chopped
7 oz. can mild green chilies, chopped
"scraps" of your favorite "veggies"
1 bay leaf   ½ t celery seed
¼ t black pepper   salt to taste
8 oz. Patchwork Pasta ★

Combine chicken breast, onion and broth in a large saucepan. Bring to a boil and simmer for 30 minutes. Remove chicken and cut into chunks. In the large saucepan (or a slow cooker), combine chicken and broth; add spices. Add any "scraps" of the following: celery, carrots, peas, corn, broccoli, tomatoes, cauliflower (fresh, canned, or frozen). The more "scraps", the better. Simmer gently for up to 5 hours. Add water if needed. Twenty minutes before serving, bring 4 quarts water to a boil. Add Patchwork Pasta. Simmer for 10 minutes; drain. Add pasta to soup and serve. Also works with turkey breast, ground beef, ground turkey or lean sausage. This "scrap soup" can be the center of a soup and salad luncheon. Check the resource section to order Patchwork Pasta ★.

Cooking can cut into precious quilting time, so a bee may prefer to eat at a restaurant instead. One bee seems to think all important decisions should be made over plates of enchiladas. They have done this so many times they are tempted to write a guide to quilt shops and Mexican restaurants in their area.

Honey Cut-Out Cookies

Makes approximately 2 dozen

½ cup margarine   ¼ cup honey
¼ cup sugar   1 egg
1 t baking powder   ¼ t cinnamon
¼ t nutmeg   ⅛ t cloves
1¾ cups flour

Cream margarine, honey, and sugar. Add egg and beat well. Mix dry ingredients thoroughly; stir into margarine mixture. Chill dough. Roll out on floured surface to ⅛" thickness and cut into desired shapes. Bake on ungreased cookie sheet at 350° for 8-10 minutes.

Honey Bees

Makes approximately 30

½ cup peanut butter
1 T honey
⅓ cup nonfat dry milk powder
2 T sesame seed
2 T toasted wheat germ
unsweetened cocoa powder
sliced almonds

In a mixing bowl, use a wooden spoon to mix the peanut butter and honey. Stir in the dry milk powder, sesame seed, and wheat germ until well mixed. Lay waxed paper on a baking sheet. Using a teaspoon at a time, shape the peanut butter mixture into ovals to look like bees. Put on the baking sheet. Dip a toothpick in cocoa powder and press gently across tops of bees to make stripes. Stick in almonds for wings. Chill in the refrigerator 30 minutes.

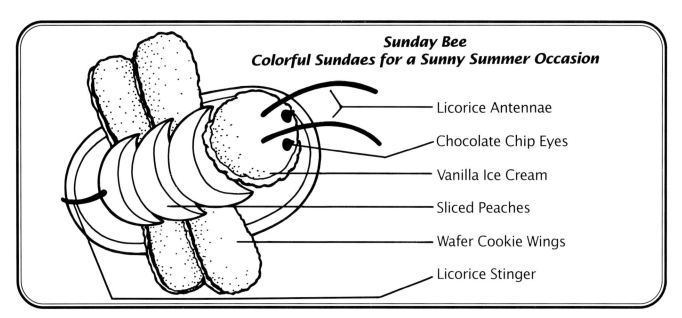

Sunday Bee
Colorful Sundaes for a Sunny Summer Occasion

—— Licorice Antennae

—— Chocolate Chip Eyes

—— Vanilla Ice Cream

—— Sliced Peaches

—— Wafer Cookie Wings

—— Licorice Stinger

 # FESTIVITIES

Bees may choose to celebrate a variety of occasions. Christmas or Hanukkah are often celebrated as well as birthdays. The beginning and end of a school year can be festive occasions for bees that have members with school-age children. Groups may want to celebrate National Quilting Day with a luncheon and guest speaker. Another group might have an annual mother-daughter tea.

One bee celebrates all the members' birthdays at one large party. A pot luck lunch is planned, and hats are brought to exchange.

Each member decorates a hat, not knowing who the recipient will be. Names are drawn, and everyone proudly displays her new designer head wear (at least through lunch).

Weddings, BEE-trothals, and arrivals of babies are certainly worthy of celebration. A bee could arrange a party for the honored member and shower her with gifts following an unusual theme such as Christmas ornaments. If the bee wants to make a special quilt, ideas can be found on pages 79 to 80.

Some occasions can be celebrated with a gift exchange. Christmas is a perfect time to exchange ornaments or holiday cookies, and fabric is always a good present for any quilter. If other gifts are exchanged, a monetary limit could be agreed upon ahead of time. A bee can plan gifts around a specific theme such as a tree; each gift has to have a tree incorporated into it in some way. Someone could make an apron using fabric containing a printed tree or quilt a pillow using a Tree of Life design. An angel, Santa, or flower might be the theme for another gift exchange.

BEE-stowing Gifts

Gifts can be exchanged in a variety of ways. Names can be drawn out of a hat weeks in advance so bee members can select a gift with a particular friend in mind, or a drawing can take place on the day of the celebration.

A fun and unusual way to exchange gifts is the exciting Steal-A-Gift. Wrapped packages are set in the center of a circle of eager bee members. Each person draws a number out of a hat. The number-one bee member selects a package, opens it, and shows everyone what she has received. The person who drew number two has the option of choosing any of the wrapped packages or "stealing" the first person's gift. If the first person's gift is stolen, she selects another wrapped gift. The third person may steal either of the two opened gifts or take any of the wrapped packages. Anyone whose gift is stolen has the option of stealing another or choosing an unwrapped package...and so on. Each round is over when someone chooses a wrapped package. Only three "thefts" can occur within one round, and after there have been three turnovers on the last round of the exchange, everyone keeps the gift she has in her hands.

OUTINGS — LEAVING THE HIVE

Part of the fun of belonging to a bee is going on outings with the group. The bee may want to go for a day trip to their favorite quilt shop, or better yet, buzz around to all the quilt and fabric shops within a reasonable distance. In the excitement of a bee's fabric-buying frenzy, a member can easily be left BEE-hind, so the buddy system may need to be used.

Sometimes there will be quilt or other needlework displays at museums or galleries, and this is another wonderful excuse to go on a trip with friends. Attending classes and workshops with bee members can add another dimension to friendships. Out-of-town symposiums or quilt shows might be exciting getaways for a quilting bee. You can be sure that bees swarm to quilt shows and make a BEE-line to the quilts!

A Quilt-Till-You-Wilt slumber party can be planned. Each member can work on her own project, or this might be a perfect time for the bee to start one of the group quilt ideas from the project section of this book. Quilt shops might let a bee use classroom space for an overnight sewing marathon. Sleeping bags and pillows can be brought by members who will be BEE-draggled by the late night hours.

If a bee can manage to get away for a longer period of time, a weekend retreat can be planned. A bed and breakfast, a condo, or perhaps a bee member's cabin could be a possible destination. Easy-to-prepare meals or visits to convenient restaurants can be planned for the weekend so there is plenty of time for sewing and visiting.

MATERIAL GIRLS RETREAT

The Material Girls Bee spent a fun weekend at a small cabin in the mountains. They wanted to spend as little time as possible in the kitchen, so they planned simple meals and ate dinners at a favorite restaurant. They also discussed snacks, and since everyone has different tastes in junk food, they each brought a large supply of their favorite snacks—enough for themselves and extra to share with friends. Several were thrilled to see a variety of chocolate set out on the table.

One member taught the rest how to stencil on fabric. She brought paint and supplies, and the Material Girls all brought their own fabrics for experimenting with the paints. One member brought a shirt to stencil and took home a nice piece of wearable art.

Just for fun, they decided to play strip poker. Before you conjure up visions of scantily clad quilters clutching cards in their hands, here is the explanation: They played a regular poker game and used strips of fabric for betting (i.e., "I'll see your two strips and raise you three strips.") Ever since the retreat they've had fun shocking others by saying that their bee has a tradition of playing strip poker!

Specialty Bees

This chapter will present the goals and activities of four specialty bees—theme bees, charitable bees, computer bees, and art critique groups. These groups have a narrower focus of interest or an unusual way of meeting, which makes them different from a "general" bee. However, one key ingredient still remains among all the groups—women sharing their love of quilting. Using some of these groups' activities or ideas may trigger new projects for your bee.

THEME BEES

A common interest in a particular quilting style may draw quilters together to form a theme bee—one where members work on a specific type of quilt. They share patterns and books that apply to their chosen theme and often use bee meeting time to teach each other specialized techniques needed to make those quilts. Members are asked to work only on projects related to the theme during bee meetings.

Some quilting styles and subjects that may inspire starting a theme bee include:
- Baltimore Album
- Hawaiian
- Christmas
- Other holidays
- Patriotic
- Miniatures
- Liturgical
- Amish

The recent resurgence of interest in Baltimore Album quilts has increased the availability of books and patterns on the subject. A bee specializing in this style will have many sources for design inspiration and may be interested in researching the history and traditions of the time. A group interested in Hawaiian quilting could rent videos on the subject and plan a luau and decorations around the Hawaiian theme.

Teaching the public about their particular interest may become a goal of the group. Theme bees might be asked to show their quilts and give demonstrations at historical sites, museums, or quilt shows. Bees can also contact libraries and schools to offer their services for teaching and demonstrating.

THE HAOLE CONNECTION

Inspired by a teacher at a local symposium, a group of friends decided to get together to make Hawaiian quilts. The group meets once a month in members' homes, and is called the Haole Connection. "Haole" means light-skinned or can be loosely translated as "non-Hawaiian". The members work on their own quilts but have been known to help other members with the tedious job of basting. They have been asked to demonstrate their craft at public service exhibits and quilt shows and sometimes arrive in Hawaiian muu-muus. Once the group met with a hula dancing class for a pot luck. The quilters taught the dancers to make pillows using Hawaiian quilting techniques, and the quilters gave the hula a whirl. A quilt made as a going-away gift was inspired by this bee and is pictured on page 56.

 # CHARITABLE — BEE-NEVOLENT GROUPS

Quilting bees can provide services to their communities through the donation of charitable or BEE-nevolent quilts. Service projects may be the main purpose for a bee's existence, while other groups may perform charitable work once or twice a year. Quilts can be donated for battered women, AIDS patients, police cars, and hospitals. Tops can be quilted on commission to earn money for donation. A raffle or "opportunity" quilt can also be used to raise funds to support local and global causes such as environmental concerns, historical restoration, and school fund-raising projects. If you can think of a needy or worthwhile cause, someone has probably made a quilt to help or commemorate it.

Spending some time investigating organizations that would benefit from receiving quilts will help the bee find the perfect group to help. The following suggestions may help begin the search.

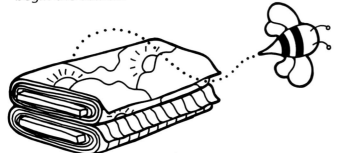

Finding Worthy Recipients

- Consult the Yellow Pages in the Social Services Organizations section.
- Ask friends about the participation of their church and/or service clubs in charitable work.
- Visit with local law enforcement agencies about their needs. Police cars can be provided with quilts to hand out to comfort children when officers assist in crisis situations.
- Consider the ABC Quilts national project to provide quilts for AIDS babies. See the resources section on page 103 for the national address.
- See if your local Ronald McDonald House needs quilts to decorate the rooms and common areas. See the resources section on page 103 for address.
- Visit or call local nursing homes. There's often a need for lap quilts made of double-knit material with ties to attach them to wheelchairs.
- Visit independent living homes for the mentally disabled to see if they have a need for quilts.
- Ask if hospital nurseries need quilts for newborns of welfare mothers.

Questions to Ask Recipients

Once the group has narrowed down possible organizations to help, asking the following questions will provide the necessary information to finalize the decision and begin the fun part of charitable quilting—the sewing. It is helpful to establish one contact person in the organization to whom questions can be directed as they arise and to whom the quilts can be delivered.

1. How many quilts will the bee need to make? Some organizations will take whatever you offer, while others may request a certain number. The request may vary from 10 to 200, depending upon the group's needs.
2. Do the quilts need to be delivered all at once, as completed, or seasonally? Some organizations only need quilts during the holidays, while others distribute quilts as they are needed.
3. If the quilts are given to a shelter, will the quilts stay on the premises or be given to families receiving help? Some shelters try to cover each bed with a permanent quilt to create a homey atmosphere, while others provide a quilt to help families set up housekeeping when they leave the shelter.
4. If donating to a church mission group, where will the quilts go? Missions can be located in the region, in other parts of the United States such as Indian reservations, or overseas. If the bee wants the quilts to benefit the local community, this question needs to be asked.
5. What size quilts are needed? Depending upon the group's needs, the bee may need to make bed, crib, lap or wall-sized quilts. Lap quilts for the elderly may need ties to attach them to wheelchairs.
6. How durable should the quilts be? Nursing homes may suggest double-knit fabrics that are easy to wash. All the quilts except those for wall decoration may benefit from machine quilting.
7. If giving quilts to a large group such as Volunteers of America, will it bother the bee to not know how the quilts are used?

For a very large organization such as the Red Cross, the bee may be unable to learn how or where the quilts are used.
8. Does the bee wish to receive publicity for their donation? Some groups are unable to publicly acknowledge donations due to the recipient's need for anonymity.

Raffle Quilts

Making one raffle or "opportunity quilt" to generate funds for a charitable purpose can also be a worthwhile project. Community fund-raising projects can help with the purchase of a new fire truck, add books to the library, supply art-reach programs, or provide trees for a park. Schools can also make quilts to raise funds for special activities. Providing funds for the Marie Webster Home Restoration which will house the Quilters Hall of Fame will promote and ensure a treasury of quilt history.

Planning a raffle quilt requires careful investigation of state laws concerning games of chance. In some states only nonprofit organizations can offer raffles, and then only after attending state-sponsored training sessions and filing proper paperwork. If raffles are legal in your area, then the bee can jump in, make a quilt, and sell tickets.

Bethany Lutheran Church women meet weekly to quilt on the frame. The funds they raise are used to purchase items on the church wish list.

Quilting on Commission

Another way to raise funds for charity is to quilt tops on commission with all of the earnings being donated to a cause chosen by the bee. Fees can be set by the number of spools used to quilt the top or by using a square-foot price determined by the quantity of quilting. The group can compile a list of tops awaiting quilting to keep the project in a continuous supply.

Acquiring Supplies

The first three or four quilts the bee makes can probably be completed using leftovers and surplus fabric from members' stashes. A bee that makes many quilts will need to plan how to keep enough supplies on hand.

Here are a few ways to inexpensively keep the project buzzing along.

- Seek a monetary grant from a quilt guild to purchase supplies or sewing machines used to make the quilts.
- Place a collection box at guild meetings for members to drop off thread, pearl cotton for tying, needles, pins, excess batting, and fabric.
- Ask local fabric merchants to save bolt ends and seconds to be collected on a regular basis.
- Ask local merchants to donate money or supplies for a raffle quilt. One shop might provide the backing and another the batting.
- Search local thrift shops for fabric or clothing that can be used in quilting.

It is suggested that for any donations of supplies, money, or time that are accepted, a public acknowledgement of the contribution be made and a note of thanks sent.

If making charitable quilts is an ongoing project, it may be helpful to meet in a large room where workers can spread out. Recreation centers and churches are often happy to have their rooms used for this purpose. They may even set aside a place to store materials and the quilting frame. For a group that makes an occasional quilt, the classroom at the local quilt shop might be borrowed for a basting session with the other meetings taking place in homes.

Ways to Make the Quilts

Making donation quilts can be accomplished by a variety of approaches.

- During meeting time groups can plan and work on one quilt at a time. When the quilt is completed, another one is begun.
- Have members make a number of quilt tops at home. Once there is an inventory of quilt tops, schedule a workday for the group to layer and tie the quilts.
- Make a Progressive Strip Quilt. This quilt has a wide variety of jobs to sign up for, from making strip sections, to taking the quilt to a professional quilter, to donating money to pay for the quilting. There is a job suited to the talents and schedule of each bee member. The directions for this charitable quilt are located on page 88.
- Teach a new strip or pattern technique at a meeting, then form an assembly line to speed-sew the tops using the new idea. Have two or three ladies ironing to speed up the process. Schedule a tying session (Tie-One-On Party) to complete the tops.

Patterns to consider for the quilt tops might include strip panels, half-square triangles, nine-patches, or split rails. Cutting novelty or juvenile fabric into 6″ or 8″ squares set with sashing can be attractive. Using simple shapes that can be assembled quickly will allow the group to create more quilts to give. The quilts being given away may not be masterpieces but will provide love and warmth to those in need.

Groups who make BEE-nevolent quilts will reap many rewards for their efforts including increased camaraderie, a sense of purpose, and the knowledge that they have helped others and our planet (i.e., recycling). 'Tis better to give than to receive!

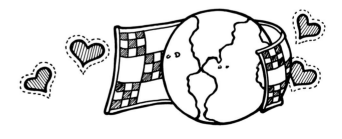

 # COMPUTER BEES

From: Sherri and Barb (BEELINE)
Subject: Quilting Bees
Sent: 6/08/93 at 6 p.m.

Dear Readers...Communicating and working with quilters across America is now possible with computer programs featuring interactive personal services. Women participate in this type of bee by leaving messages on the computer for other members, which they retrieve up to a week later. Many of the projects and friendships developed in local weekly bees are possible through computer "bee" membership.

Benefits of participating in this type of bee:
- Making quilting friends across the country. Sharing ideas from different regions offers exposure to new trends in quilting.
- Participating in a group without the need to attend weekly scheduled meetings. This is helpful for working women, as they can squeeze in this activity when time permits.
- Never having to dress up for meetings. Designer pajamas and curlers are just the ticket. No need to be BEE-dazzling!
- Providing opportunities to network with other quilters if isolated in a rural area, frequently relocating, or homebound. Women who frequently relocate because of corporate and military careers only need to plug in the computer in order to continue communication with computer quilting friends.
- Having an immediate response to questions or ideas.
- Ability to select which projects are of interest and whether to participate in a group project without hurting other members' feelings.

To join a computer bee, all that is needed is a computer, telephone access, and membership in an interactive computer service. Services to consider are listed in the resources section. Membership is open to anyone interested in quilting who has basic computer knowledge. Dues are not collected for bee membership, but expenses might be incurred for the computer service fee, long-distance phone expenses, and postage for mailings. Each member can choose her level of participation. Volunteer leaders/hosts provide an organizational structure to the group projects.

Computer bee activities are similar to those of local bees. Discussing quilting ethics, copyright laws, quilting techniques and styles, and developing teaching contacts might be posted under topic headings. If a topic is of interest, one may read the comments about the topic and may enter the discussion by posting additional ideas. Discussion of personal matters occurs under the heading of "chatter". This heading serves as a way to create a personal link with other members, if desired.

The main difference from a local bee is how group projects are handled. Because of the members' varied geographic locations, projects will need to be mailed. Computer bees have successfully completed progressive border rotation quilts, blocks of the month, fabric swaps, and charitable quilts. These projects use guidelines similar to those explained in the project section of this book.

The task of planning and coordinating group activities for members spread across the country requires special considerations. A proposed activity may have hundreds of potential participants. Each proposed activity is posted on the computer bulletin board by a leader/host (the originator of the idea), and members may place their names on the sign-up list. Participation in a project may be limited to a specified number or open to all who are interested. Sign up is generally open for a few weeks or until the allotted positions are filled. The leader may then divide the sign-up list into small groups with an appointed liaison, post the lists on the bulletin board, and let the sewing begin. Another approach is to have the host receive all of the projects or fabric, handle the sorting, and then send the packets back to the participants. The costs of mailing are handled by each participant; return postage is included in the packets sent to leaders for redistribution.

FIELD OF DREAMS

At the National Quilting Association Show in Davenport, Iowa, sessions were scheduled for computer bee members to meet each other in person and discuss issues related to quilting and computers after many months of electronic communication. As an extra bonus, activities were planned for a small group of quilters who had discovered a second common interest (passion), baseball, while visiting on Prodigy. Tee-shirts, caps, and a special excursion to the Field of Dreams created an additional link of friendship for this group that calls itself The Field of Dreamers. It's reported that baseball quilts are in the works.

Activities Over the Wires

Below are listed some computer bee activities and how the organization of each is handled.

▼ *Block of the Month Drawing*

The leader posts a block description on the first of the month. A noncopyrighted block is chosen that can be found in a popular quilt book. Anyone may sew a block and then post her name on the board. The leader randomly selects and posts a name to receive the blocks that will be mailed from the participants. The winner becomes the next leader and selects the next block. The cycle continues in this manner.

Unique to block of the month drawings in computer bees is the possibility of using E.Q., Electric Quilt. This program allows the user to design and draft a block on the computer. Members can then print this design and instantly have all the pattern pieces and directions. The winner can be chosen as above.

▼ *Stone Soup Swap (Thematic Fabric Swap)*

Participants send the leader packets of fabric that fit the chosen theme. Stone Soup includes meat and vegetables (fat quarters) (see page 81), seasoning (one 10″ square of zinger fabric), and a stone (bag of scraps right off the worktable). After receiving the fabric, the host sorts and swaps it and mails a packet back to each participant. Sewing can then begin with a new assortment of fabrics to include in a quilt.

A Hey, Diddle, Diddle swap can feature cow, cat, and moon fabrics with a dish or a spoon thrown in for good measure. Brainstorming can lead to other theme swap ideas such as Tropical Paradise or Home on the Range.

For women in isolated areas or small towns with few shops featuring quilting fabric, these fabric swaps serve as an important source for exposure to new and unusual fabrics available in other areas of the country.

▼ Birthday Fabric Club

All that is needed to BEE-long to this club is a willingness to send a fabric gift to each of the participants on her birthday. The group agrees on a uniform size of fabric to send, usually a fat quarter. Throughout the year fabric is sent to each member on her birthday. Once the participant's birthday rolls around, fabric will arrive from all of the other club members. Imagine receiving 42 un-BEE-lievable fabrics, as one member did.

▼ Block Exchange

Block exchanges in computer bees can include more participants than a local bee, as the number of members is not limited to a home's seating capacity. The leader can plan a quilt with a set number of blocks and post a sign up tailored to meet those needs. If a common fabric is desired, the leader mails it to each participant. At the end of the month, completed blocks are mailed to the leader so she can assemble them. The next hostess now posts her desires for the block exchange. The cycle continues until each person receives a set of blocks.

▼ Group Quilts

Computer bees can make group quilts similar to those listed in the project section. A leader may propose an idea and purpose for a group quilt. Once the blocks are complete, assembling and quilting the top can be done by one volunteer or by a professional quilter hired by the group. The Miles Apart Dollmakers Doll Quilt on page 35 is a group project made by doll enthusiasts across the country. These group quilts can be used for any of the purposes listed in the section on charitable bees.

▼ Real Time Conferences

Quilting authors and designers are invited to present a lecture or discussion to be presented on the computer. Members can all "listen in". Following the lecture all the members may join in the conference by posing questions for the lecturer to answer.

Joining a computer bee might open the door to many new quilting friendships and ideas. Just BEE-ware—it can be addictive. Now two interests, quilting and computers, will demand your attention.

ART CRITIQUE GROUPS

A discussion of specialty bees would not be complete without including art critique groups. These groups do not necessarily label themselves as "bees", but they certainly fall into our definition since they gather friends to share information and support their quilting endeavors. The purpose of an art critique group is to evaluate members' work and offer suggestions to help them grow as artists. Meeting with a group can counter the feeling of isolation sometimes experienced by artists who work alone in studio settings.

Membership

These groups are comprised of quilt artists who meet to encourage each other and are committed to promoting quilts as an art form by displaying their works in art shows and gallery settings. Members wish to further their art studies, and most wish to sell their quilts. They usually view themselves as professional artists who happen to make quilts, and they strive to move beyond tradition or beyond craft in their quilting. Many art quilters have come to fiber arts from painting, sculpture, pottery, and other art fields.

The groups we interviewed limit membership from eight to twelve in order to keep the group intimate and allow every member to show at least one quilt in group exhibits. Membership is by invitation with some groups requesting a résumé and slides of the prospective member's work for evaluation prior to extending an invitation. Most groups receive more requests to join than space allows. Prospective members need to show a commitment to exploring quilt making as artistic expression and an interest in pushing beyond traditional approaches.

Activities

The majority of the art critique groups we interviewed meet once a month with the location rotating among the members' homes. Sessions include the sharing of information about upcoming quilt shows, new techniques learned in workshops, and reviews of books on art theory and creativity.

The main activity of these groups is critiquing the artists' work. They are encouraged to bring to each meeting a completed quilt or one that is in progress. Members comment on the merits of a design and may offer suggestions to improve weak design elements. Sometimes an artist reaches a difficult stage in making a quilt and can benefit from others' ideas.

Meeting time can be used for discussion about topics of interest to the group. Subjects can be planned ahead with members taking turns presenting information to the group and leading the discussion.

Topics to consider:
- Color theory
- Design elements
- Creativity
- Arranging efficient workrooms
- Developing professional portfolios and résumés

Some groups ask all the members to make a project following a particular theme. This will create a related body of work for exhibits. It is always interesting to see how different individuals interpret the same topic. Humor as a theme is portrayed by quilt artists on pages 58 and 59.

Some suggestions for theme projects:
- Landscapes
- Floral inspirations
- Letters, numerals, or symbols
- Reflections
- Song Titles
- Discovery
- Texture
- Ethnic Influences

Some groups use these ideas only as sources of design inspiration and do not require members to complete thematic projects. Others have abandoned the idea of project assignments and encourage members to pursue independent work and develop individual styles.

Exhibitions

Many critique groups approach art galleries to arrange shows for exhibiting members' work. A gallery may want to see a portfolio containing members' résumés and slides of their quilts as well as a list of past exhibits. Galleries that specialize in displaying fiber art can be found in listings in art magazines, phone books, or by asking other fiber artists. Before making a commitment to a gallery, members need to know what the group's responsibilities are and what is provided by the gallery.

These subjects should be addressed in a legal contract:
- Will the gallery make arrangements for a reception? Who pays for it?
- What publicity does the gallery provide?
- Does the gallery furnish invitations? How many? Who pays for postage?
- Does the gallery have its own mailing list for invitations and publicity? Can the group add its own list to the gallery's?
- Who will do the hanging, and what equipment is furnished by the gallery? Do quilters need to supply their own hanging rods?
- How will the quilts be sent to the gallery and returned? Who pays?
- What commission does the gallery take on sales? When will the artists receive payment?
- What insurance is provided by the gallery for individual quilts? What is the total insurance coverage for all the quilts in the show?
- Will someone be on duty all the time? Can the gallery space be locked?

Piecemakers and Quilt Explorations gather to share ideas and offer encouragement at a joint meeting.

Libraries, offices, and public buildings often have spaces that can be used for art exhibits. Check phone books for local government listings or visit spaces that have previously shown artwork. Any show will incur some costs, and the group may want to collect dues to cover expenses.

Networking

Some of the groups we interviewed have joint meetings with other art critique groups. This provides an opportunity to see other artists' work and studios and to discuss topics together. Two art critique groups might meet twice a year to share ideas and visit over a pot luck salad luncheon. A Christmas get-together can include an ugly fabric exchange with each member bringing equal-sized pieces of ugly fabric for every other member. They can challenge each other to use all of the uglies in one project. Two members met this challenge, and their BEE-guiling quilts can be seen on page 47.

HELEN'S CRITIQUE GROUP

Once each month since 1980, Dr. Helen Davis, a retired fine arts professor, has generously opened her home to a variety of artists to offer them encouragement and advice in their artistic endeavors. This unusual critique group began when a handful of weavers, wanting to learn more about design, asked Helen to teach classes. Helen declined but said that she would be glad to host an informal seminar-type get-together in her home. The group remains very informal with no officers, minutes, or dues.

This interactive group is attended by artists working in all mediums—painters, sculptors, weavers, and potters, as well as quilters. Participants have come and gone, and some have returned working in a different medium. Helen has remained the fearless leader and mentor.

From time to time, the group surprises Helen with handwoven clothing or other handmade "goodies". The quilt on page 56 was given to her as a thank-you gift.

Quilt Gallery

A Sailing We Will Go, My Friends and I. By Sharon West and Parker Bag Ladies, 1993, Parker, Colorado, 49½″ x 52½″. For her birthday Sharon received boat blocks of various sizes and challenged herself to set them together with Ocean Waves. She trimmed a little here and added a little there to get them to fit. This project is machine quilted mostly with freehand techniques using rayon, metallic, and nylon threads. Some of the block patterns are from *Nautical Voyages for Quilters* by Betty Boyink.

On The Street Where You Live. By Alison Schwabe and the Friday Block Party Bee, 1988-1993, Colorado, 32″ x 104″. Alison, a native of Australia, says about this quilt made from exchange blocks, "Every house is different. To my eyes they are all so very American and therefore a great reminder of the bee at that time. Some have moved away but will never be forgotten. I myself expect, one day, to move back to Australia. This quilt will go with me as a wonderful memory of friends and good times in the bee."

Friday Block Party Building Quilt. By Barb Lister and the Friday Block Party Bee, 1988-1993, Colorado, 71½″ x 72¼″. To set her exchange blocks together, Barb added a variety of amusing novelty prints in the sashing between buildings. A salt box house by the ocean has Columbus' ship docking on one side and hungry sharks lurking below, while cowboys and Indians surround the Mexican restaurant in the desert. Barb even found a clock button to sew to the peak of the courthouse.

Miles Apart Dollmakers Doll Quilt. By Marilyn Jeppson and Miles Apart Dollmakers, 1993, 64″ x 84″. Blocks in this quilt were made by 23 doll makers from all over the US. Most participants are not quilters and have never met each other in person but became acquainted through the Prodigy computer service. Marilyn requested quilt blocks with a doll theme on the computer bulletin board and offered to assemble and finish the quilt. The dolls are embellished in every way imaginable.

Simply A Sampler. By Carol Savage 1992, Denver, Colorado, 56″ x 56″. A pattern exchange in the Great American Quilters group was the inspiration for this quilt. Each month a member of the group brought a different pattern for a 6″ block. Carol hand pieced the entire quilt.

Guardian Angels. By Connie Klunder and Homestead Friendship Sampler Bee, 1992-1993, Colorado, 56″ x 64″, detail. Connie chose a pattern from *Always Angels* by Nancy Smith & Lynda Milligan for her Member of the Month block exchange. Painted faces and sky background fabric were given to each member.

Button Christmas Quilt. By Marilyn Jeppson and Buttonhead Prodigy Group, 1992, Colorado, 23½″ x 17½″. Wishing to swap buttons, this group of women decided to make 5″ Christmas blocks each embellished with five buttons. Marilyn put her blocks together in this small quilt to display the group's unsurpassed imagination and talent.

Love Quilt. By Never Enough Quilts bee for Phyllis A. Oliver, 1991, Colorado, 59″ x 70″. This quilt was made for Phyllis by her bee members to give her comfort and support during a difficult time in her life. The quilt's title reflects all the loving stitches sewn into the quilt. Pattern ideas are from Judy Martin's *Scraps, Blocks and Quilts.*

Amish Hands All Around. By Paula J. Neufeld and Parker Bag Ladies, 1990 and 1993, Parker, Colorado, 38″ x 38″. The Bag Ladies make blocks for each member as a birthday gift. Paula chose the Hands All Around block and asked the members to make it using Amish colors. She created the border with scraps left over from the blocks. Paula says, "Much to the chagrin of the group, the more time that passed, the more elaborate and complicated the blocks became, but it was a great way for everyone to develop more skills in drafting, stitching, and designing."

Amish Adventure. By Carol Savage and The Great American Quilters, 1991-1992, Denver, Colorado, 64″ x 64″. The Great American Quilters chose 8″ Amish blocks for their 1991 block exchange. Each of the participants made 24 identical blocks, one for herself and one for each of the 23 others. The blocks were exchanged in December, and in January Carol set them together and pieced a border using the same colors.

Colorado Memories. By Barb Lister and friends from three bees, 1992-1993, Colorado, 69½″ x 78″. When they heard that Barb was moving, her friends organized an unusual kind of friendship quilt. Guidelines were loose enough to allow each participant to make a block reflecting her own personality or her special relationship with Barb. Any shape or size block was allowed, and a narrow range of colors helped tie the varied shapes together. They knew that Barb loves puzzles and would have fun assembling the blocks.

Over the Edge Quilters gathered a bevy of Remember Me Blocks. Members were amazed at the colorful display. Inspired by Colorado Memories on page 39, odd-sized blocks were chosen to represent something special in each member's life. Some of the patterns this group used are found in the pattern section.

Colorado Friends. By Chris Brown and Over the Edge Quilters, 1993, Littleton, Colorado, 74″ x 74″. "It was a tremendous challenge to assemble odd shaped blocks in a harmonious setting. Also, I had no idea purple, yellow, teal, and lime green could look so good together!" Chris designed an unusual diagonal background and added additional small blocks.

Hands In Mine. By Mary Beth Church and Over the Edge Quilters, 1993, Littleton Colorado, 60″ x 53″. At first Mary Beth was unsure of her ability to assemble different-sized blocks. She worked out her design on graph paper and was so pleased with the result she immediately called several bee members to see if they wanted to do the same project again!

Colorado Friends. By Judy Kraus and Over the Edge Quilters, 1993, Littleton, Colorado, 54″ x 54″. Judy planned her quilt on graph paper before she began sewing. She has used trees and stars in many of her other quilts, so she decided to fill in this quilt's odd spaces with small versions of her favorite blocks. The schematic for Judy's quilt can be found on page 65.

Remember Me. By Leslie Lott and Over the Edge Quilters, 1993, Englewood, Colorado, 50″ x 52″. Leslie asked for solid Amish colors for her blocks and said about her project, "This is the most fun I have ever had making a quilt!"

Bees in the Friendship Garden. By Sherri Driver and Barb Lister, 1993, Colorado, 63″ x 75″. While brainstorming for this book, the authors realized that a bee quilt would be a charming addition. Nine-patch flowers made of friendship fabrics are interspersed with buzzing bees. The garden is contained by a beehive border, and a queen bee presides over the swarm. Pattern on page 83.

Hidden Hearts. By Barb Lister, 1993, Highlands Ranch, Colorado, detail. By adding a few extra pieces to the album block used in the Friend-zee quilt on page 44, Barb created a whole new shape. Can you find the heart? The blocks can be arranged in a variety of settings to create secondary designs. Pattern on page 92.

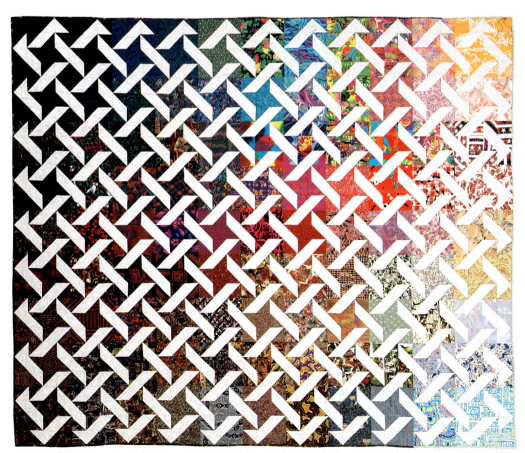

Friendship Stars. By Judy Kraus, 1993, Littleton, Colorado, 85″ x 105″. Judy has always loved the traditional Friendship Star block, and her arrangement of the colors gives it a contemporary look. Ninety-nine different fabrics were used—all of them gifts from friends.

Stars of Friendship. By Mary (Sandy) Sanford, 1993, Littleton, Colorado, 57½″ x 73″. Each star in this quilt is made of four fabrics representing four different places or occasions. Sandy's quilt contains all of the bee's friendship fabrics for 1992.

Buzz Saw. By Chris Brown, 1993, Littleton, Colorado, 65″ x 65″. Chris had fun working with fabrics unrelated in color. She was surprised to discover that purple could be used as a neutral to tie the odd colors together. The signature blocks were inspired by ideas presented at a calligraphy workshop given at an Arapahoe County Quilters meeting.

Friend-zee. By Sherri Driver, 1993, Englewood, Colorado, 76″ x 87″. An autograph block with muslin strips (pattern on page 91) was chosen to feature messages and pictures from bee members. Sherri's goal was to make the colors move across the quilt. Large pattern pieces show off novelty prints.

Kalispell #1. Mary K. Ayres, 1993, Aurora, Colorado, 53″ x 38½″. Mary K. had taken a class on bargello quilts shortly before participating in a strip exchange. She thought it would be a fast and easy project but found out the hard way that mistakes on the serger take more time to undo than mistakes on the sewing machine!

Strips Around The World. By Leslie Lott, 1993, Englewood, Colorado, 49½″ x 49½″. Following printed directions, Leslie thought she was sewing one large Trip Around the World block but was surprised to end up with two small blocks instead. She sliced one into four pieces and came up with this arrangement.

Just Peachy. By Beth Bishop, 1993, Littleton, Colorado, 37″ x 37″. Beth worked with the Child's Delight block because she had never seen it used before. When choosing a name for her quilt she looked for a play on the word delight and was reminded of a former boss who always claimed that things were "Just Peachy!"

Mother's Day Friendship Sampler. By Judy Kuhn and Mother's Day Quilters, 1979-1993, Georgia and Colorado, 95″ x 110″. The blocks for this quilt were secretly taken from Judy's home, so Chris Brown could complete the top as a gift to be presented at the annual Mother's Day Quilters retreat. She made five additional blocks and then assembled the blocks and borders.

Friendship Cabin. By Pat Thompson and Mother's Day Quilters, 1986-1993, Georgia, 58″ x 75″. After relocations from Georgia to Germany to Georgia and then to Milwaukee, Pat vowed to complete this quilt as a tribute to the Georgia bee members' support and love through unsettling times. Note quilt to the left—similar blocks-different settings-different look!

Sister's Choice. By Judy Manning and Friendship Sampler Bee, 1989, Colorado, 58″ x 70″. For Judy this quilt celebrates many firsts, first year in Colorado, first year in a bee, and first year as a quilter. She selected this pattern, provided the neutral background, and asked for peach and blue for her turn in the Member of the Month Block Exchange.

Fantastic Fish. By Janet Robinson, 1991, Colorado, 31½″ x 25½″. Janet designed her piece using machine appliqué and a pieced border. Ugly fabrics are enhanced with the use of acrylic and squeeze-bottle paints splattered about the top.

With Help From Friends. By Anne Theobald, 1992, Colorado, 30″ x 32″. Anne wished to explore an improvisational style after studying with Sue Alvarez and Nancy Crow. Fabrics from ugly exchanges and Anne's scrap box were used to make four blocks of a simple pattern. No templates or rulers were used, and work progressed quickly and joyfully with any mistakes viewed as a creative surprise or "psychic designing".

Bag Lady's Delight. By Phyllis Jeffrey and the Parker Bag Ladies, 1993, Colorado, 53″ x 53″. On the second border rotation, a friend appliquéd an orange cat to the star to remind Phyllis that she had helped her pick out a real orange cat, a revered pet. Other appliqué reflects aspects of Phyllis' life.

Friendship Hearts. Left. By Lucy Poppe and Piece Corps, 1989-1993, Colorado, 43″ x 43″. Lucy beautifully combined eight heart blocks that she received during her first block exchange. A ninth block inspired by Christal Carter in her book *Holiday Happenings* was added by Lucy. Centering a block made on point, adding viney appliqué, and framing the individual blocks added interest. Blocks were exchanged on Valentine's Day.

Donna Cook's Personal History Quilt. Below. By Donna Jeanne Cook and Never Enough Quilts bee, 1989-1990, Colorado, 59″ x 77″. As the Member of the Month, Donna planned for each member to make a different block which reflected a significant event in her life. Donna says she chose the patterns and fabric with more freedom because this quilt was the first made to please just herself. Many of the blocks were chosen from *Judy Martin's Ultimate Book of Quilt Block Patterns*.

Friendship Baskets. By Sherri Driver and the Wednesday Bee, 1991-1993, Colorado, 62″ x 79″. The Wednesday Bee chose the popular basket pattern as a monthly block exchange. Baskets were made in the colors chosen by the recipient of the month. Sherri selected green baskets and created a special triangle design to surround the quilt.

Cake Stand Baskets of Friendship. By Sandra Durham Smith and the Wednesday Bee, 1991, Colorado, detail. Sandra's quilt commemorates many firsts—bee, block exchange, and friendship quilt. Muslin squares contain signatures of dinner and house guests, friends who made blocks, and the hand prints and footprints of her five grandchildren. This will be a wonderful treasure and record for future generations.

Black Beauty. By Georgeen Goodell and Tuesday Nite Bee, 1993, Colorado, 42″ x 42″. Beginning with an appliquéd center square, this quilt ended its rotation with an unusual shape. Members added borders, nine-patches, and extra triangles, as well as appliqué vines and hearts.

The Biblical Flood. By Mary (Sandy) Sanford and The Over The Edge Quilters, 1991, Colorado, 41½″ x 27″. Sandy's rotation top began with the dove block. Each member added sections that reflected Mary's chosen theme, the Biblical Flood. The olive branch was added to the dove's mouth during the Persian Gulf War, and the rainbow reflects hope for the future.

A Child's Winter in Colorado.
By Carol Medsker and Tuesday
Nite Bee, 1993, Colorado, 31″ x
31″. The beginning block included a little girl building a
snowman. There was no snow on
the ground, so on the first
rotation a snow field was added.
The cozy winter scene took
shape with an ice skater gliding
across a pond. The scene is
enclosed by checkerboards on
two sides.

**With A Little Help From My
Friends.** By Nancy Sorce Kruziki
and Tuesday Nite Bee, 1993,
Colorado, 41″ x 41″. Nancy began
her rotation with four of the pret-
tiest blocks from an unfinished
sampler quilt begun five years
earlier. Bee members added the
central block and surrounding
triangles. Hearts, a wreath, and a
dove were appliquéd throughout
the rotations. Borders complete
this lovely wall quilt.

Celebration of Children's Literature. Above. By Mary G. Shatwell and Tuesday Nite Bee, 1993, Colorado, 36″ x 26″. As a teacher of first and second graders, Mary chose to have her rotation reflect a favorite classroom book. *Each Peach, Pear, Plum,* by Janet and Allan Ahlberg is an "I Spy" type of book where readers find children's literature characters. Mary placed the book in her rotation bag so members could read the story before making additions. The quilt will be used as a teaching aid in the classroom.

New Directions. Left. By Kathy Nicklas and the Parker Bag Ladies, 1993, Colorado, 51″ x 51″. To begin this border rotation, Kathy and her husband, Ted, designed a Mariner's Compass to depict their hope to build a boat. Intricately appliquéd anchors enhance this nautical theme. Bits of orange and yellow portray sunshine shimmering across the blue water.

Country Winter. By Kathy McClintic and Tuesday Nite Bee, 1993, Colorado, 33″ x 24″. Kathy's rotation began with a charming bundled boy surrounded by a one-inch checkerboard border. Members added five additional appliquéd squares, removed the checkerboard, added strips of appliquéd hearts, and reattached the checkerboard border. This quilt depicts the simple joys and pleasures of wintertime in the country.

Here's To The U.S.A! By Cheri Hurd and Tuesday Nite Bee, 1993, Colorado, 53″ x 38″. A tea-dyed flag set the theme for this patriotic rotation quilt. Members added five red, white, and blue blocks featuring appliqué and piecework. Cheri feels the activity was uplifting—sharing the love of quilts with friends and helping each other with different techniques.

Progressive Strip Quilt. Designed by Emmy Midkiff and made by Sherri Driver and Barb Lister, 1993, Colorado, 65″ x 91″. The Patchworkers bee uses this quilt pattern for charitable quilt projects. The quilt pattern and unique way of completing it are located on page 88. This quilt is a duplicate of one the group gave to a local women's shelter.

Tennessee Waltz. By Janet Jo Smith and Friday Block Party Bee, 1989, Littleton, Colorado, 69″ x 87″. Over a year, the members of the Friday Block Party Bee made exchange blocks for each other. When Janet's turn came, she selected Tennessee Waltz and gave bee members tan fabric to use in each block for uniformity. Janet asked for navy stars and scraps in the rest of the block. She made additional alternate blocks to finish the quilt top. Pattern in *Scrap Quilts* by Judy Martin.

Off The Deep End. By Over The Edge Quilters, 1992-1993, Colorado, 80″ x 84″. This theme rotation is a play on names of fish. Photo transfers were used to enhance some ideas—Marilyn Monroe's head is sewn on a starfish. An electrical plug is attached to the electric eel. Paint, metallic thread, and decorative objects are used to embellish this quilt.

Another Great Day. By The Wednesday Designers for Helen Davis, 1991, Boulder, Colorado, 88″ x 88″. Diana Bunnell designed the three-piece block and coordinated the making of this quilt as a thank-you for Helen's willingness to host an art critique group in her home. Two of the three basic pieces for each block were cut and distributed by Diana, and members of the design group used the third piece to create a special work of art. When a forest fire threatened her home, Helen was faced with the question, "What does one take when a house is about to burn down?" This quilt is so special to her that it ranked third on the list.

Hawaiian Echoes of Friendship. By M&Ms for Emmy Midkiff, 1993, Colorado and Texas, 56″ x 56″. When Emmy's bee learned of her upcoming move, they planned a quilt that Emmy had said she would love but never make due to its huge amount of appliqué. The label for this quilt is shown on page 80.

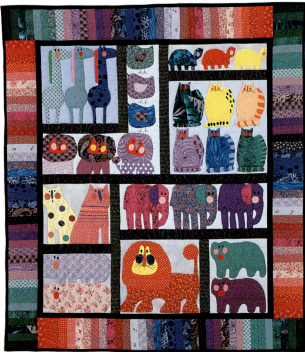

A Rainbow Over Jeffrey's Zoo. By the Parker Bag Ladies for Cheryl Lassen, 1991, Parker, Colorado, 37″ x 43″. This wall hanging was made to celebrate the birth of Cheryl's son. Each Bag Lady appliquéd a different animal block. The pattern is *A Rainbow Over My Zoo* by Anna Holland.

Farewell Santa. By the Sunbonnet Sue Bee for Pat Rogner, 1991-1992, Illinois, 49½″ x 61″. Good friends created this rotation quilt for Pat upon her move from Illinois. The Santa is a variation of a Cindy Taylor Clark design, and the border was designed by LaVerne Larson. LaVerne taught many in the group to quilt and shared her love of quilting and appliqué with the group. Memories of dear friends abound in this quilt.

Far Side of the Garden. By The Over The Edge Quilters, 1991, Colorado, 52″ x 37″. Humor abounds in this quilt which portrays names of flowers through a visual presentation of plays on words. A snapdragon is depicted by sewing snaps on a dragon shape, while an eggplant is made of fried egg blooms. Embellishments include plastic bugs and chenille bumble-bees. This quilt is a theme rotation project and includes work by each bee member. It was a juror's prizewinner at the 1991 Denver Botanic Gardens Quilt Show.

"How Many". By Christine L. Scott, 1991, Parker, Colorado. The writings in Tom Robbins' *Jitterbug Perfume* inspired this humorous theme vest for an art critique session. Robbins answers the medieval theological question about angels dancing on the head of a pin by posing another: "It all depends, are they jitterbugging or dancing cheek to cheek?" Chris visually presented these ideas by using machine appliqué, hand embroidery, hand beading, and hand quilting.

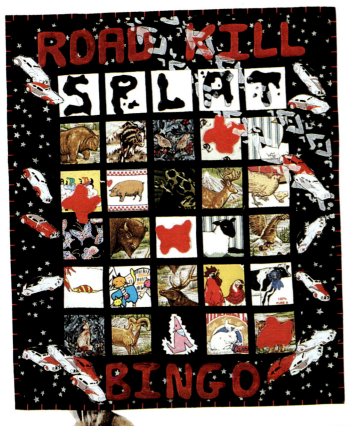

Roadkill Bingo. Left. By Barb Lister, 1991, Colorado, 19½" x 23". Made as a humorous project in an art critique group, this is Barb's reaction to a Christmas marketing campaign featuring the perfect gift for family car trips, Roadkill Bingo. Wouldn't every family delight in finding this game under the tree? Pushing this morbid idea are the painted tire tracks, splat-shaped game markers, and a wild array of animals.

PMS. Below. By Sherri Driver, 1992, Colorado, 36" x 36". Sherri captured the frantic, wild feelings of PMS in this humorous quilt made in an art critique group. The intricate face, wacky lamé hair, and bloodshot eyes portray the sleepless nights and out-of-sync feelings many women experience. Caffeine cravings are depicted by a coffee mug and chocolate treats.

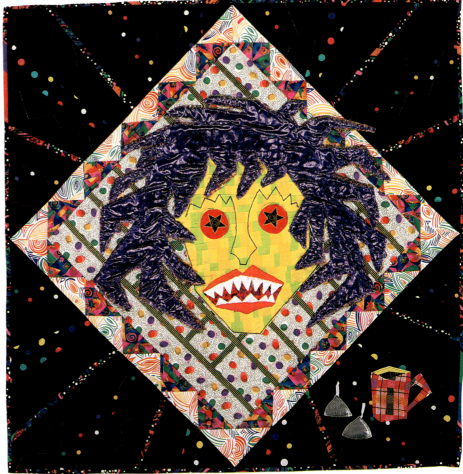

Projects for the Swarm

One of the joys of bee membership is participating in group projects. Groups can make collaborative quilts, share fabric, trade patterns, participate in challenges, and exchange blocks. Each project can involve all of the members and build camaraderie and enthusiasm.

As the bee undertakes many types of exchanges, members may wish to keep a record of the blocks and projects they have made and for whom. The chart on page 16 is one type of record. As the years go by, this record will document the members' names and also show how much the group is accomplishing.

To enrich your quilting experiences, to create interesting and unique quilts, and to keep the bee buzzing, give one of the following projects a try!

 EXCHANGES

An exchange is the giving and receiving of items such as blocks, fabrics, or patterns between bee members. Planning exchanges ensures that bee members will have a token of each member's friendship without having to move or get pregnant! These exchanges might be considered as projects just BEE-cause they are fun to do. The Remember Me blocks will provide an opportunity to make blocks that reflect the maker's personality or a special relationship with the recipient.

Block Exchanges

Blocks made by friends can be a treasury of memories and can inspire special quilts. Block exchanges involve giving and receiving completed quilt blocks. The timing of giving the blocks can differ. One member can be honored each month with blocks made by fellow bee members, or blocks can be BEE-stowed on all the members of the group at once.

▼ *Member of the Month—Block of the Month*
Each month one member can be the recipient of blocks of her choice. She selects or designs a block that she would like members to make for her and provides them with patterns and instructions for making the block. A color recipe (see page 64) or a common fabric can be given and used in all the blocks. Each member can be asked to make a different pattern to create a sampler quilt, or all the members can make the same block. The recipient needs to be specific about what type of quilt is planned. It is helpful to provide the guidelines in writing.

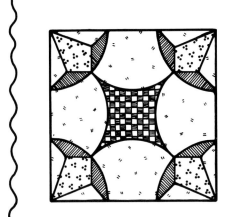

I'm looking forward to getting my blocks at the end of this month. Since I will be getting these in November, I thought that the Turkey Tracks block would be great. I have drafted the block to be 8″ when finished. I know that a few of you have never pieced a curved seam before, so I would be glad to teach you at the next bee. I've included a beige print for you to use as the background, and I would like the other fabrics to be any autumn colors. Call me if you have any questions.

Happy Quilting,
Suzie

After assembling the quilt top, a label can be designed documenting the blocks' names, why the blocks were selected, and who made them. This label can be sewn to the back of the quilt. Donna Cook's Personal History Quilt is a result of the Member of the Month idea and is featured on page 48. Her label appears below. (The December Days block is at the bottom left corner of the photo.)

DONNA COOK'S PERSONAL HISTORY QUILT

December Days	Pride of Ohio	Valley of the Sun
Donna was born in December	She was born & lived her early years in Ohio	She lived in Phoenix as a teenager
Pieced by Melody Whittemore	Pieced by Donna	Pieced by Laurie von Holdt
Hoosier Block	**Sparks Flyin'**	**Star Sapphire**
Donna met Jim, from Indiana, in high school	The relationship between them was special	Jim gave Donna a star sapphire for graduation
Pieced by Suzanne Haley	Pieced by Beth Parvu	Pieced by Terri Nugent
June Bride	**Prairie Nine-Patch**	**Mother's Day**
Jim & Donna were married in June	She was exposed to skills of prairie homemakers	Their 1st child, a boy, was born
Pieced by Phyllis Oliver	Pieced by Roma Brown	Pieced by Donna
Wash. Monument	**Boy's Nonsense**	**Denver Mint**
The family moved to the D.C. area	Their 2nd child, another boy, was born	The family moved to Colorado
Pieced by Laurel McKahan	Pieced by Sherrie Wilson	Pieced by Doris McAllaster

Here are some ways that the recipient of the blocks can be selected:
- Random drawing. Draw names out of a hat. Assign members' names to months in the order drawn.
- Birthdays. Members receive blocks during their birthday month.
- Alphabetical order.

A group can simplify the block exchange idea by choosing one pattern that will be made each month by all the members and given to one member a month according to a predetermined schedule. For example, the May Basket block can be chosen as the exchange block for the entire year. The recipient can ask for certain colors, but the block for that year remains the same. This is a great time saver for people who like to make their blocks all at one time, and the pattern needs to be drafted only once.

Another twist on this idea is to have the group choose a block design and color scheme. Each bee member makes one block. When they are done, one name is drawn out of the hat, and she is the lucky winner of the set of blocks. Once a member has won blocks, her name is omitted from the drawing until all the others have had a chance to win. Members are expected to contribute blocks for the remainder of the drawings until everyone has a set.

Going one step farther with this idea, one bee has each member make a block, and then the group assembles the blocks, hand quilts, binds, and sews on a label. Their goal is to finish the quilt in time to enter the county fair. After the quilt is finished, a name is drawn to determine the lucky winner of the completed quilt. It has been reported that many times the Thursday Night Therapy group (TNT) has been up all night finishing the last stitches to meet the fair deadline. Surely this an isolated incident. Your group certainly wouldn't wait until the last minute!

Choosing which type of block exchange and when to swap should be discussed at the bee. It is helpful to think about members' schedules and skills to make the best selection for all the members. If the group includes beginners, making the blocks can serve as minilessons. Would it be difficult to make blocks for each member that are due all at the same time, or is it best to spread the block-giving throughout the year? Appliqué projects might require a longer period of time to complete than patchwork. Selecting a block, individualizing blocks, and using color recipes can all be considered.

▼ Mass Exchange

Block exchanges can be arranged so that everyone receives blocks on the same day. The group needs to agree on guidelines and a time line. The time needed to complete the blocks depends on the complexity of the design and the schedules of the participants. Each member makes identical blocks for all the other members and herself. This project lends itself well to theme ideas such as:
- Houses or buildings
- Dolls
- Christmas or other holidays
- Ships
- Patriotic blocks
- Angels
- Hearts
- Cats

Theme quilts made from block exchanges are found on pages 34, 38, and 48.

A special bee meeting can be planned for the big exchange day. Receiving blocks from bee friends can be as exciting as getting birthday presents. After swapping blocks, members can begin sharing ideas and planning how to assemble their friendship quilts.

▼ Ideas for Assembling Exchange Blocks

Same-size blocks are easiest to assemble into quilt tops. Here are some suggestions for putting exchange blocks together:
- Sew sashing or checkerboards between blocks.
- Add a plain or simple pieced block between exchange blocks.
- Set blocks on point and add interesting set-in borders. Friendship Baskets on page 49 has used this approach.
- Set blocks side by side. Amish Hands All Around on page 38 is set this way.
- Create a quilt with an unusual shape to fit in a special place. The long quilt on page 34 is designed to fit in an upstairs hallway.

A quilt top can be made larger by:
- Making more blocks yourself.
- Adding an alternate plain or pieced block between the exchange blocks. Tennessee Waltz pictured on page 54 uses this idea.
- Adding wide or multiple sashing between blocks.
- Setting blocks on point.
- Adding multiple borders.
- Combining blocks from two bees, if a member belongs to more than one group.

Blocks made by different individuals may vary in size. If so, try:
- Trimming blocks to the size of the smallest block.
- Adding framing strips all around the blocks to bring them up to a uniform size.
- Taking blocks apart and remaking them.
- Choosing a random set or arrangement where the block size is not important. The Miles Apart Dollmakers Doll Quilt on page 35 and the heart quilt on page 48 successfully combine blocks of many sizes and orientations.

Once the blocks are exchanged and assembled into quilt tops, it is exciting to see how the projects vary. The quilts made by Mother's Day Quilters, on page 46, include similar blocks yet look entirely different because of the setting arrangement and the use of additional blocks.

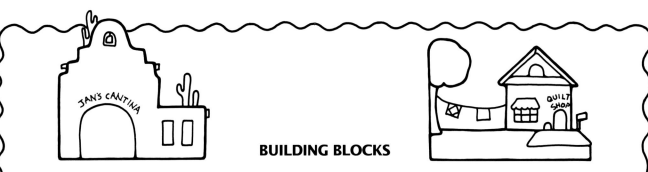

BUILDING BLOCKS

Once again members of the Friday Block Party Bee wanted to exchange blocks among themselves. After a weekly meeting they adjourned to the group's favorite Mexican restaurant to discuss a new project— Building Blocks. The idea was to choose a building with a special meaning for the maker. The lawyer in the group chose a courthouse and incorporated a Courthouse Steps block as the stairs. Of course, one member chose a Mexican cantina to reflect the many times the group had met over plates of enchiladas. It is still a mystery why one member selected a barn, since she was raised on military bases and in cities. (She says that every town should have a barn. BEE-wildering!)

Two months after the planning session, the members gathered for an exchange party. Special refreshments were served, cameras readied, and anticipation rewarded with a wide range of blocks. As thrilled as they were to receive their blocks, it became apparent that the blocks were going to be difficult to assemble. Twelve inches had been the finished height of each block, but the scale of the blocks varied immensely. (One-story to four-story buildings were all represented as 12″ tall.) Also, muslin was the agreed-upon background, but the group soon realized blue would have been so much prettier.

One year later a brave member arrived at the bee with her top assembled. It was charming and inspiring. One by one the other members began to assemble their blocks into tops. Additions to the blocks included goofy theme fabric such as sharks and sailing ships for the seaside cottage, and coyotes and vaqueros herding cattle around the Mexican cantina. Novelty buttons such as a clock were added to the courthouse tower. Trees and shrubbery were added to soften the scale differences and to make the rows a uniform length.

The problems encountered with the set of blocks were solved using creativity and humor. Photos of two of these quilts are located on page 34.

▼ Remember Me Block Exchange

If bee members enjoy designing blocks and are willing to accept a challenge, a group might have fun breaking out of the square block format. Each participant can choose a traditional block, or she may design one that represents something special about herself. A caffeine addict may choose to make coffee cups, or someone who travels might make Mariner's Compasses. Blocks can be made in multiples of three inches (or substitute multiples of two inches), and they can be square or rectangular. Rectangular blocks can be designed to be placed vertically or horizontally. Each member will receive a recipe card from each of the other members and will then sew her own block design in all of the requested color combinations. A bee with ten participants will produce ten different blocks made from ten different color combinations for a total of 100 blocks—no two alike. **Un-BEE-lievable!**

To make a color recipe card, attach snippets of fabric to sturdy paper and give one to each member as a guideline. The following color recipe card was given to bee members to guide them in choosing fabric for a block exchange.

▼ Odd-sized Blocks

Assembling blocks of various shapes and sizes into a quilt top can be challenging, but the results will be well worth the effort.

Suggestions for assembling odd sized blocks:
- Plan the layout on graph paper. Cut rectangles and squares accurately representing the size of each block in the quilt. (One square of graph paper can equal one inch.) These paper pieces can be moved around on a large piece of graph paper until a pleasing arrangement is made. Spaces between the blocks can be filled with plain fabric, strip piecing, or other pieced sections.
- Shapes with equal sides can be sewn together and odd spaces filled with plain or strip-pieced fabrics.
- Plain or pieced framing can be added to small blocks to bring them up to the measurement of larger blocks.
- Some blocks can be broken into smaller units and sprinkled throughout the quilt.
- Make additional blocks to add to those received. Colorado Friends by Judy Kraus, on page 41, uses this idea. She used graph paper to determine the layout for her blocks. Friendship stars, trees, and checkerboards are added to this quilt.

COLOR RECIPE CARD

Please include two or three of these colors in the block you are making for me. I'd like the blocks to reflect a flower garden.

ROSE

BLUEBELL

GOLDENROD

HONEY GOLD

THIS KIND OF RECIPE SURE BEATS THE COOKING KIND!

Here are the blocks Judy received:

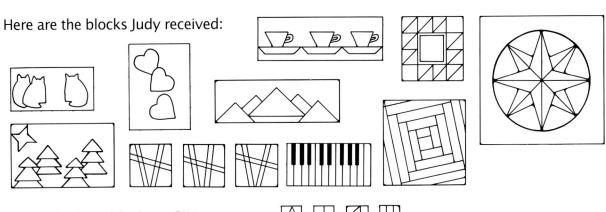

She made these blocks to fill in spaces:

Here is the schematic of Judy's quilt. She played with these elements on graph paper and came up with this arrangement.

Pattern Exchanges

A monthly project to consider is a pattern exchange. Members can select a month in which they present a pattern and its directions to the bee. At the next monthly meeting members can have a show and tell of blocks using the previous month's patterns. The next pattern can be handed out by another bee member. A pattern exchange can be used as an opportunity to learn drafting, piecing, or appliqué techniques. An experienced bee member can serve as a mentor and guide the group through challenging patterns. The sampler quilt by Carol Savage on page 36 is the result of a pattern exchange.

Patterns to exchange:
- 6″ blocks
- Santas
- Calendar blocks
- Blocks with a patriotic theme (eagles, flags, and Uncle Sam)
- 12 Days of Christmas
- Challenging patterns such as Jinny Beyer's

Fabric Exchanges

Fabric exchanges are BEE-witching because all quilters love fabric and are often on a mission to obtain more. Some clever ideas have resulted from attempts to create more variety in the fabric stash or to acquire that 999th piece of fabric for a charm quilt.

Choosing to exchange fabric allows bee members to sew their own projects rather than make blocks for others. An exchange of fat quarters (18″ x 22″) or fat eighths (9″ x 22″) will give bee members sufficient fabric to make a variety of pieced or appliquéd blocks.

Smaller squares or other shapes can also be exchanged. Squares cut 6″ or 4½″ can be used for scrap or charm quilts and can be cut into other shapes as desired by the participants. Here are some ideas for those squares:
- Slice them diagonally and use the resulting triangles.
- Cut them into four equal squares and add another fabric for nine-patches.
- Cut them into rectangles.
- Use each one as the center of a block.

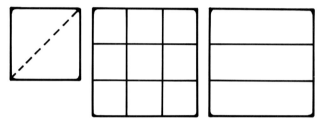

Exchanging fabric cut into other shapes can be the BEE-ginning of another fun project for the bee. Here are some shapes to consider:
- Rectangles—2½″ by 6½″ pieces are the perfect start for a Stacked Brick quilt.
- Diamonds—60˚ diamonds can be made into a variety of six-pointed stars, Baby Blocks, or Inner City quilts; 45˚ diamonds will make a Lone Star or other eight-pointed stars.
- Circles—great for yo-yo projects like Christmas garlands.
- Triangles—equilateral triangles can be made into Thousand Pyramids, hexagons, and projects using 60˚ diamonds.
- Hexagons—can be made into Grandmother's Flower Garden.

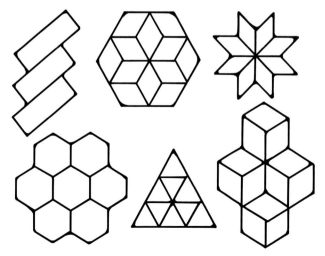

Distributing templates of the shape chosen will help keep the swap fabrics a uniform size. Even with a template, expect some variance in size due to individual cutting techniques.

These exchanges can be geared to a certain type of fabric such as blacks, florals, or stripes. It's amazing to see the variety when the fabrics are pooled. It might be suggested to include fabrics in equal amounts of dark, medium, and light values. The bee needs to decide if all fabric should be 100% cotton and if the fabrics need to be prewashed.

Strips of fabric can be exchanged and may inspire many different projects. The group needs to decide on colors, width of the strips, and a day for the exchange to take place. Strips can be limited to a few colors, or a wide range of fabrics can be chosen for a scrappy look. The quilts featured on page 45 use this idea.

In the next column is an example of how to make the guidelines clear to each bee member. Also, if a bee member is absent the day the project begins, a handout will clarify any questions.

The Never Say Die Quilters Strip Exchange

This exchange will be lots of fun because so many different quilts can be made from strips. Here are a few examples:

Log Cabin
Nine-Patch
Double Nine-Patch
Radiant Nine-Patch
Rail Fence
Bargello
Mock Log Cabin
Lone Star
Trip Around the World
Many Trips Around the World

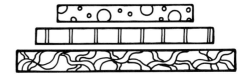

Please follow these guidelines:
- Cut strips of print fabric 2″ wide from selvage to selvage so the strips will be 2″ wide by 44″ or 45″ long.
- The strips are to be peach and blue fabrics and prewashed 100% cotton.
- Select six different fabrics, two darks, two mediums, and two lights. The wider the variety of fabrics, the more interesting the scrap quilt will be (florals, stripes, geometrics, novelties).
- Cut ten strips of each of the six fabrics, one for each of the other nine bee members and one for yourself. About ⅔ yd. of each fabric will be needed. When the cutting is complete, you will have 60 strips.
- Come with strips cut in two weeks, April 12, for the exchange.
- Let's try to enter the guild's challenge this fall!

STRIP EXCHANGE CUTTING GUIDE

Use this chart to figure the number of strips necessary to make a wall quilt.

Number of bee members:	Each member will need X different fabrics.	Cut 2″ strips from the following for each member:			Number of different strips after exchange:
	X	lt.	med.	dk.	
5	15	5	5	5	75
6	12	4	4	4	72
7	9	3	3	3	63
8	9	3	3	3	72
9	9	3	3	3	81
10	6	2	2	2	60

CHALLENGES

A challenge can be a fun and exciting activity for any bee. Its purpose is to push the members' capabilities and stimulate them to try something new. A challenge is a set of guidelines that each member follows and can be as simple as the required use of a specific fabric or as complex as a rigid set of rules. Whichever approach a group decides to take, a challenge can help it expand its quilting horizons. Several types of challenges are available—fabric, shape, technique, color, theme, or personal. Each one will present a different set of learning situations. Your group can pick and choose from the ideas listed below and create a customized challenge that suits the skill level and desires of the bee.

Fabric Challenge

The use of a particular fabric can be the starting point for a challenge. The group decides on one specific fabric that must appear in the quilt top, and that is the only rule. The bee can take a trip to the local quilt shop and choose the fabric that will be common to all the projects. This can be the hardest part of all! With the one fabric as the sole requirement, participants are limited only by their imaginations. Some variations on this fabric challenge:

- A packet of coordinated fabrics chosen by the bee. The requirement may be to use each of the fabrics in the packet or any specified number of them.
- A predetermined type or style of fabric such as a plaid, stripe or lamé. Participants are allowed their choice of fabrics as long as they stay within the guidelines.
- A fabric from a specified designer or company such as Hoffman, P&B, or Jinny Beyer.

The bee might want to participate in a prearranged challenge such as the one sponsored by the Hoffman fabric company. A specific Hoffman print is required in the

project, and the participant purchases it herself. This annual event has become so popular that just finding the fabric can be a real challenge in itself. Send for the rules and entry form for this challenge by writing to the address indicated in the resources section of this book.

A fabric challenge does not have to be planned around beautiful fabrics. Interesting projects can be inspired by an ugly fabric or a group of uglies. Most quilters own fabric that makes them wonder if their minds were controlled by aliens when they picked it out. Each bee member can bring a fat quarter of something she considers a real "dog", trade it for someone else's "pooch", and challenge others to make a project using friends' rejects. If everyone has large pieces of uglies, they can be cut and distributed so that each member can be challenged to work with an identical packet of ugly fabrics. Bee members will probably discover that one person's trash is another's treasure. Two projects using uglies can be found on page 47.

Shape Challenge

A group may want to forego the idea of using the same fabric and choose another focus for its challenge. Selecting a shape for the outside of the quilt or the pieces within the project might be an interesting twist to the challenge idea. Here are some shapes to consider:

- Circle
- Diamond
- Hexagon
- Square

Technique Challenge

Trying a new skill might be an exciting stimulus for a challenge. Perhaps members have learned interesting techniques in books or workshops and are ready to apply these new skills to a quilt. Your group might consider planning a challenge around any of the following techniques:

- Appliqué
- Curved seam piecing
- Strip piecing
- Painting and stenciling
- Embellishing
- Pleats or tucks

Color Challenge

A group can issue a challenge based on using a specified color or color scheme such as:

- Monochromatic (light, medium and dark versions of one color)
- Black and white only
- Complementary colors (two colors that are opposite each other on the color wheel such as red and green)
- Full spectrum (all the colors of the color wheel)

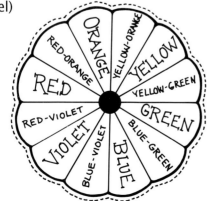

Theme Challenge

A particular subject or theme can spark ideas for a challenge. It is always exciting to see how different people interpret the same theme. Bee members are sure to have ideas to add to the following list.

- Memories
- Humor
- Holidays
- Ethnic
- Americana
- Cats
- Seasons
- Greeting card or painting as inspiration
- Reflections (realistic or retrospective thoughts)
- Over-under-around-and-through (intertwinings or individual interpretations)

Personal Challenge

Each bee member can issue an individual challenge to herself to complete a project, try a new technique, or use colors that are new or difficult for her. A deadline can be chosen for the declared challenge to be completed and shown to the rest of the group.

The projects on pages 58 and 59 represent a humorous challenge with no size limitations. The strip exchange quilts located on page 45 can also be designed as challenge projects.

Cross Pollination of Ideas

A challenge can be a combination of any of the above ideas. For an Americana theme, participants could use striped or plaid fabrics, while another bee may choose to make monochromatic, humorous quilts with strip piecing. Possibilities are endless, and the results are as varied as the personalities of the participants. Remember, there are no right or wrong results in a challenge!

To Plan a Challenge

Group members should jointly discuss and agree upon the rules and timetable for the challenge. When making up guidelines, consider the following:

- The skill level of the members. It should be challenging to all the members but not so far beyond anyone's ability that frustration sets in.
- The time required to complete the project. Make it short enough to keep it interesting but long enough to be reasonable.
- Secrecy. The day the challenges are unveiled will be more exciting if no one has previously seen them.
- Showing of the challenges. This could be done ceremoniously, honoring each participant and congratulating her for meeting the challenge!

It might be helpful to give the guidelines of the challenge to the bee members in written form. Following is one example.

HAPPY HOOPERS SPRING CHALLENGE

Spring will be here before we know it, and we could all use a cheerful new wall hanging, so let's all make a Spring Fever challenge.

- *Make your quilt 24″ x 24″*
- *Use at least 3 of the following spring colors—pink, peach, yellow, green, blue, lavender*
- *Add any other colors you want*
- *Use a floral theme—floral prints, appliqué or piecing*

Bring your finished quilt to the March 20 bee. We are planning our annual Spring pot luck lunch that day.

Our favorite quilt shop would like to display our challenges for the month of April, so be sure to get your project done!

 ROTATIONS

Creating rotation quilts is an interesting way for a group to work together. A rotation quilt is one that has gone through a cycle of changes as each bee member individually plans and carries out alterations to a beginning quilt section. This exercise encourages improvising with new colors and techniques, requires knowledge of basic quilting skills, and produces unpredictable results.

The major difference between the two types of rotations that follow is the number of quilt tops produced. If each member wants her own quilt top, choose the Brown Bag Rotation. Try the Theme Rotation to produce one quilt top for the group to complete.

Brown Bag Rotations

This enticing project combines secrecy and spontaneity and produces a quilt top that includes work by everyone in the group. A brown bag rotation project begins as a block or quilt section made by one member. It progresses with other members adding to or altering it in some way.

To begin this project, each participant needs to prepare a block or section for her quilt. The initial block can be a pieced or appliquéd quilt square, the beginning of a scenic background, or a beautiful piece of dyed or stenciled fabric and can be any size or shape.

Each bee member writes the first entry in a journal that will be passed along with the quilt top to each of the other members. Including a journal gives the originator the opportunity to let her friends know if she has specific ideas for her project. She may have a particular color scheme, finished size, or theme in mind. The beginning blocks and the journals are placed in brown paper bags.

A special bee meeting needs to be scheduled for the brown bags to be ready and distributed. Plan enough time for each person to show her beginning quilt section, read the introduction to her journal, and have a photo taken of her project. These pictures will serve as a reminder of the original appearance of the quilt top. This is the last time the projects will be seen by the entire group until everyone has had a turn to "do her own thing" to each of her friends' projects.

The bags are now ready to begin their journeys. They are passed in turn to each participant, and she will decide what changes and additions will improve the quilt top. Once the sewing, painting, or embellishments are complete, snap a photo of the altered quilt top and write comments in the journal. Each member can write about what she did to the top and why. When everyone has done "something" to all of the quilts, the bags will return to their owners. An "unveiling" party can be planned to view all of the quilt tops, pass out the photos to help recreate the quilt top's evolution, and celebrate the project's conclusion.

Some suggestions for the beginning of a rotation are:
- Dramatic blocks forming a center medallion
- Blocks left over from a sampler
- A collection of old-fashioned blocks made by a real or imaginary "auntie"
- A hodgepodge of orphan blocks and abandoned projects

A rotation project can have a theme such as a story or a setting. Bee members might have ideas to add to the following list:

- A favorite children's storybook
- A biblical or historic story
- An ocean or mountain scene
- An empty room

A rotation does not require a preconceived theme. A bee member might want to turn her friends loose to do anything they want to her beginning block. Giving fewer guidelines at the start of the project allows each participant to use her own creativity, and the finished project will be more surprising. The colors and shapes in a project might suggest a theme to a participant. A journal entry can encourage others to further develop that theme. A bee might decide to forego the secret aspect of this project and allow everyone except the owner to see the block and make suggestions. This is especially helpful for beginning quilters who may not know which choices to make. In this way the project can be used as a learning experience, and patterns as well as techniques can be shared.

RENÉE'S STORY

The first entry in J. Renée Howell's journal told this story: "My best friend's Great Aunt Nell recently died and left the enclosed quilt blocks and material to her. She doesn't know a pin from a needle, and she has asked me to make a quilt top so she will always remember her Great Aunt Nell." The brown bag contained blocks in a variety of sizes and colors and several pieces of old-fashioned fabric. There were 8″ variable stars, 6″ nine patches, and 4″ pinwheels.

As the project was passed around, other members wrote about the imaginary Great Aunt Nell as if they knew her too. Since the Aunt Nell idea was so cute, another bee member invented Aunt Francine to help her select and sew buttons on the hearts of Aunt Nell's quilt.

How can a quilt top be altered?
- Add plain, pieced, or appliquéd borders.
- Add triangles to set a block on point.
- Cut apart and reassemble (also known as slice-and-dice).
- Appliqué.
- Paint or stencil.
- Add pleats.
- Make a fancy label and attach it to the quilt top. Some of the quilts on pages 51 to 53 feature cross-stitched labels.
- Add buttons, sequins, ribbons, or other BEE-dazzlers.
- Make additional parts, toss them in the bag, and let someone else figure out where they go.

▼ Moving the Bags BEE-tween Members

The bags can be rotated among bee members in alphabetical order. Members' names can be written on the bags and crossed off as each member completes her alterations to the project. With this method of rotating bags, participants will receive a bag from the same individual each time and always give it to the next person on the list.

Bags can be rotated randomly rather than in a definite order. Each member writes only her own name on the bag. Names or numbers can be drawn from a hat to determine who takes which bag home for alterations. One group throws bags into the middle of a table, and the participants just grab another bag, making sure they have not chosen their own. If someone ends up with a project she has already worked on, she just trades for another.

WINTERSCAPE
by Sandra Durham Smith
The following drawings show how Sandra's quilt evolved as it moved from member to member in a brown bag rotation.

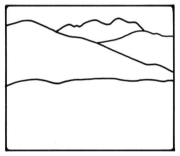

1. Beginning.

2. Trees and sun appliquéd.

3. Lake and more trees added.

4. Skaters, cabin and tree added. Chimney smoke embroidered.

5. Bridge and sledder added. Stream added so bridge does not float at end of lake.

6. Two outer borders completed the rotation quilt.

TRANQUILITY
by Charlene Oswald
The following drawings show how Charlene's quilt evolved as
it moved from member to member in a brown bag rotation.

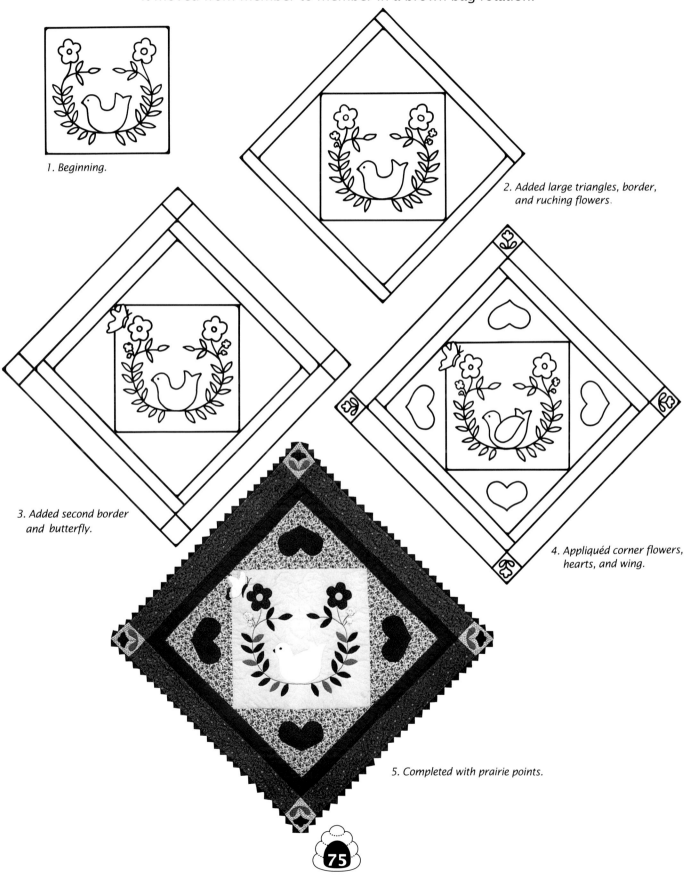

1. Beginning.

2. Added large triangles, border,
   and ruching flowers.

3. Added second border
   and butterfly.

4. Appliquéd corner flowers,
   hearts, and wing.

5. Completed with prairie points.

▼ *Variations*

A group might want to apply stricter rules to rotation projects.

- Border Rotations—Each participant can be asked to start with a block of a specified size, and the other members can add borders using any technique. Borders could be pieced, appliquéd or stenciled.
- Scheduled Technique—Members can start with a block of their own choice, and as the block is passed along, other members make changes using a predetermined schedule or list of techniques. For example, everyone might be asked to appliqué on the first rotation, stencil or paint on the second, and cut apart and reassemble it on the third. Quilts using border rotations and scheduled techniques, by Phyllis Jeffrey and Kathy Nicklas, appear on pages 47 and 52.

▼ *Guidelines*

Rotation quilts can be tailored to the bee's personality and skill level. While one group might be interested in trying new techniques, drafting patterns, and creating unusual quilts, another group may feel more comfortable making traditional quilts or making additions that can be borrowed from or inspired by printed patterns. Snowbound and The Evergreen Quilt inspired parts of the quilts on pages 51, 53, and 74 by Carol Medsker, Kathy McClintic, and Sandra Smith.

It is helpful to decide on a timetable. Two weeks between rotations will keep enthusiasm fresh and seems a reasonable amount of time to make an addition to a quilt top. The timetable and order of rotation can be printed for each member.

To avoid hurt feelings, it is suggested that your group agree that no member can completely cover or remove another's work.

After months of sewing, bee members will look forward to a special unveiling party. The journal entries and revealing comments that follow show just how much emotion and enthusiasm can be generated by rotation projects.

JOURNAL EXCERPTS

"Sorry I didn't do much on your top, but you know I'm getting ready to move. I just sewed on a few buttons — 5, one for each of my grandchildren."

"Do I really have to do the 'A' word-applique?"

"I tried to make it not so symmetrical."

"During dinner I described to George the project we were undertaking and how we were to take chances - do something different - you mean "Samurai Quilter," he said. No inhibitions."

An appliquéd teddy bear was the inspiration for Kathy Mihm-Dunning's rotation quilt. She thought her group, the Tuesday Nite Bee, would enjoy working with a children's theme.

REVEALING COMMENTS

"I woke up this morning and hit my husband and told him, 'Today's the day we get our quilt tops back!'"

"This is so fabulous! I love the little birds."

"Who put on the sequins?"

"This is so much better than I ever imagined!"

"I can't stand it! I can't stand it! It's so wonderful!"

"Who did these prairie points?"

"At the beginning this was so frightening that I almost quit. But by the end I was always excited to see each new top so I could figure out what to do with it."

"I hate doing checkerboards!"

"Who made these wonderful snowflakes?"

"You all did such intricate things!"

"I appliquéd a piece there, I took it off and appliquéd it over there, then I took it off again and appliquéd it over there. I didn't like it there either, so I took it off again. All I ended up with was a hole over there!"

"It's so sad that it's all over. Let's do another project."

Theme Rotation Quilts

A theme rotation can be just as fun and challenging as any other group project. This quilt project differs from the Brown Bag Rotation in that only one quilt will be produced. It would be perfect for a bee that needs to make a gift quilt or wants to enter a contest that has a group quilt category. The bee decides on a theme, makes one background or beginning section, and each member takes a turn making changes or additions to the quilt top. Possible themes are a vegetable garden, a roadway with cars, an empty room, or outer space. The quilts on pages 55 and 58 are theme rotations with a humorous approach.

▼ Hints

Consider these points when planning a theme rotation to avoid a BEE-wildering situation.

- Decide on a time line that rotates the quilt quickly and concludes the project in two to four months. This will keep the bee buzzing.
- Place large items on the quilt first. If there will be overlapping items, be sure to leave some ends loose for the next seamstress. (BEE-sides, she'll like you for that!)

- Discuss ownership of the quilt upon completion.
- Discuss how expenses will be shared among the members.
- Photograph the quilt top's progress frequently to record its evolution.
- Create an interesting backing with a label including title, participants, date, and any stories associated with the quilt.

FROM THE EDGE OF THE GARDEN

Learning of a quilt show at the Denver Botanic Gardens, the Over the Edge Quilters decided to create a humorous quilt to display with all of the BEE-utiful floral designs that would be entered. Puns and plays on words of floral names became the theme. Each member went home and pored through gardening books and encyclopedias searching for unusual plant names. Bee time was spent "weeding" out floral names that had a nasty or offensive connotation and visualizing how to sew the flowers so the play on words could be easily understood. Novelty fabrics were used to portray images that were difficult to sew. A fox cut-out was appliquéd to a real glove for the foxglove flower, and a trout was added to the center of a lily to make the trout lily. One member used a kitchen dish rag to create the ragweed.

One bee session was spent assembly-line sewing the brick background. Next a minilottery took place to decide which flowers each member would create.

Panic was now setting in as only two months remained before the contest deadline. The group decided to rotate the quilt every four to five days depending on which members were in town and did not have company. Flowers were added where each member thought they fit best, and if over- or underlapping was needed, the sewing was left loose. Surprisingly, no master drawing was ever made. Now, that is blind confidence in your friends!

While the quilt was being made, everyone looked for unusual embellishments to add to the top. After five weeks the top was completed, and the goofy plastic ants, glow-in-the-dark bugs, and chenille bumble-bees were added.

Winning a second place ribbon and seventy-five dollars was the icing on the cake after all the fun of creating the quilt. The prize money and the fact that there was only one ribbon became the BEE-labored topic of the next bee meeting. What to do? After much BEE-moaning it was finally decided to duplicate the ribbon, so each of the participants would have one for her brag wall. The remaining money was used to start another humorous rotation quilt. This prizewinning flower quilt is pictured on page 58.

SPECIAL TIMES SPECIAL PEOPLE QUILTS

Quilters have always made projects to commemorate special occasions. Births weddings, anniversaries, birthdays, going-away mementos, and thank-yous are reasons to make a group quilt for someone special. A healing quilt can also cheer up a friend who is ill or suffering through a death or divorce in her family. These quilts will show a member how much she is appreciated and loved by her fellow bee members.

To Make a Quilt

If your group wishes to make a special quilt for someone, here are some ways to get started.

- Make a Progressive Strip Quilt as described on page 88 and shown on page 54.
- Select a published pattern and have each member make a portion. The baby quilt on page 56 is an example of this approach.
- Decide on a block size. Each member may then choose any block that fits the pre-scribed size.
- The carte blanche approach: Each member can make a block of any size using pre-determined color guidelines. The blocks can be chosen to reflect something unique about the relationship between the maker and the recipient. A shared experience, a favorite food, a collection, or even a love of animals can be a design inspiration. Colorado Memories on page 39 is an example of this style.
- Choose a theme to portray such as hearts, animals, flowers, or blocks whose names suggest a certain subject or geographic region. Make the blocks the same size.
- Choose an all-over appliqué pattern and rotate the quilt top among the bee members. The Santa quilt on page 57 was made this way.

Bees Joining Together

For some occasions, if the recipient belongs to two or more bees, it might be fun and productive to coordinate one large, special quilt. One person will need to serve as a liaison between the groups to create a cohesive quilt. Colorado Memories on page 39 is the combination of three bees' work.

Using a color recipe (guideline) can give the quilt uniformity for a pleasant overall appearance. The group can choose a sashing fabric or a group of fabrics to include in each block to tie all the blocks together. It is helpful to hand out a swatch of fabric or a card with snippets of the fabrics to be included in the quilt to each member.

To Quilt or Not to Quilt

Groups need to consider whether they will complete the entire quilt or present a set of blocks for the recipient to arrange. It's helpful to think about why the quilt is being given. A going-away quilt that is unassembled may provide hours of pleasure for the recipient prior to her meeting quilting friends in her new location, while a baby quilt that is unassembled may lay in a box for quite some time due to the new mother's lack of time.

One of these ideas may help accomplish the quilting.

- Pass the quilt from member to member on a weekly schedule.
- To maintain the surprise factor, present the finished top, and then place it in a frame for all to quilt on as a group.
- Collect money from each member in order to hire a machine quilter.

Special Labels

As the years go by, it may be difficult to remember exactly who made which block and the pattern's name. Placing a label on the back of the quilt will document this information as well as tell for whom, why, and when the quilt was made. The following label, designed by Cindy Russell, was included with the Hawaiian blocks shown on page 56.

For Emmy Midkiff...♥...♥...♥...♥...

Maria Slingerland BLUE JADE	Shirley Wegert ORCHID	Jann Hoffman Ti LEAF
Jan Albee PLUMERIA	Sylvia Druckenmiller WOOD ROSE	Rosemary Angelos HOYA
Mary Jane Cook BREADFRUIT	Janet Lyles MAILE	Cindy Russell TORCH GINGER

With Love from M&M Quilters
Denver, Colorado   April 13, 1993

It is rewarding to make someone feel so special and loved.
What better gift can be given than a quilt from friends!

WRAPPED IN LOVE

Phyllis received a Love Quilt at a special bee held in her honor. Her friends explained that whenever things were difficult or frightening she should wrap herself up in the quilt and know that she is loved. She describes this quilt as one of her greatest treasures, as it offers not only warmth and beauty, but also loving support from friends.

FRIENDSHIP FABRICS

This type of group project differs from a fabric exchange as it involves *giving* fabric rather than *exchanging* fabric. When a member returns from a trip, she might bring a fat quarter of a fabulous fabric as a gift for each bee member. Being delighted to receive such a perfect gift, bee members on future trips can reciprocate by searching for just the right friendship fabric to purchase for each member. As this tradition catches on, each member's fabric stash will multiply at an un-BEE-lievable rate.

The idea of presenting fabrics from travels can be expanded to giving friendship fabrics for any conceivable reason from thank-you gifts to just BEE-cause gifts. They can even be used as wrapping paper for other gifts! It's often hard to repay someone with money after a favor has been accepted, but payment in the form of fabric will seldom be refused. In essence, friendship fabrics can become "Legal tender for all debts, public and private."

These special fabrics are important enough to set aside and save for projects commemorating friendships. The quilts on pages 42 to 44 are created from friendship fabric collections.

Personalizing blocks or quilts made from friendship fabrics will preserve memories forever. Quilts can be planned with blank spaces for writing. Collecting signatures of friends, dates, names of cities in which the fabrics were purchased, poems, drawings, and sayings can all add special meaning to a quilt. Use permanent marking pens for preserving these precious memories directly on the finished quilt.

What are fat quarters and fat eighths?

- A fat quarter is a half-yard of fabric split along the fold line with each piece measuring 18″ x 22″. Each yard of fabric will yield four fat quarters.
- A fat eighth is a fat quarter split in half vertically or horizontally depending on the fabric design. Each piece will measure 9″ x 22″ or 11″ x 18″. Each yard of fabric will yield eight pieces.

Fat quarters and fat eighths are workable sizes to give as friendship fabrics. Many shops have fabrics this size already cut and wrapped in a BEE-guiling way. Both sizes are also easy to cut from yardage at home. As the stacks of friendship fabrics grow, the group may decide to change the size of gift fabric from a fat quarter to a fat eighth. This is more economical, and many patterns can easily be cut from a fat eighth.

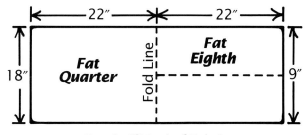

One-half Yard of Fabric

Ways to Use Friendship Fabrics

- Make one group quilt using all the friendship fabrics given over a certain time period.
- Divide the fabrics into categories of color, value (light and dark), or style, and make two or more quilts from the resulting groups of fabric.
- Make challenge quilts (see page 69).
- Select a common neutral color for the background such as muslin, black, white, or gray to help control the hodgepodge of colors and designs.
- Choose a block such as Autograph (page 91) or Hidden Hearts (page 92) that includes a blank area to feature personalizing. See photos on pages 43 and 44.
- Make a quilted gift for the giver of the friendship fabrics, and the fabric will have gone full circle!
- Stash it!

THIRTEEN EIGHTHS = ONE YARD?

Carol, a member of a small quilting bee that had been giving friendship fabrics to one another, began to feel a bit guilty that she had received so many pieces of fabric but had not given any. When her family finally planned an out-of-town trip, she was very excited at the prospect of buying fabric to share. Breezing around the store, she spotted a beautiful piece of material that everyone would love. As she set the fabric on the counter, she realized that it might be tricky to figure the amount of fabric to buy so that each person would receive a fat eighth. Asking the clerk for a little help with the math seemed reasonable. When asked, "How many eighths are in a yard of fabric?", the clerk scratched her head and replied, "I don't know right offhand, but I'll figure it out." After scribbling for a few seconds, the clerk replied, "Thirteen. There are thirteen eighths in a yard of fabric." Fortunately, the fabric was so wonderful that Carol purchased extra for her personal stash which more than made up for the clerk's faulty math!

BEE-utiful Patterns

BEES IN THE FRIENDSHIP GARDEN

Designed by Barbara Lister and Sherri Driver

Finished Size 63″ x 76″
Finished Block Size 12″

Yardage (42″- 45″ wide)

Blocks

white	2¾ yds.
yellow (bee bodies)	½ yd.
gray (bee wings)	⅔ yd.
black (bee heads)	⅛ yd.
bright scraps	19 pieces 2½″ x 13″

Sashing

white	1⅛ yds.
purple	⅛ yd.

Borders

white	1 yd.
purple	1⅛ yds.
Binding	⅝ yd.
Backing	4⅔ yds.
Batting	81″ x 96″

Cutting

Blocks

white	80 B, 80 Br, 80 E, 1 I, 1 Ir, 1 L, 76 squares 2½″ x 2½″, 80 rectangles 3½″ x 6½″
yellow	80 A, 1 H
gray	80 C, 80 Cr, 1 J, 1 Jr
black	80 D, 1 K
bright scraps	95 squares 2½″ x 2½″

Sashing

white	49 rectangles 1½″ x 12½″
purple	30 squares 1½″ x 1½″

Borders (no patterns given)

white			
	Q	18	1½″ x 10½″
	S	18	1½″ x 8½″
	U	18	1½″ x 6½″
	W	18	1½″ x 4½″
	Y	18	1½″ x 2½″
purple			
	X	18	1½″ x 11½″
	Q	4	1½″ x 10½″
	V	18	1½″ x 9½″
	S	4	1½″ x 8½″
	T	18	1½″ x 7½″
	U	4	1½″ x 6½″
	R	18	1½″ x 5½″
	W	4	1½″ x 4½″
	P	18	1½″ x 3½″
	Y	4	1½″ x 2½″

Binding	7 strips 2½″ x width of fabric

Directions For Assembly

1. Piece 80 small bees. Appliqué bee heads (D) on piece E before sewing to bee body.

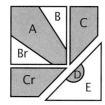

2. Piece one large bee. Appliqué bee head (K) onto piece L before sewing to bee body.

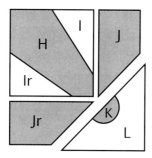

3. Piece 19 nine-patch blocks with white and bright scrap 2½″ squares.

4. Assemble 19 blocks with nine-patch centers and 3½″ x 6½″ rectangles. Stitch the small bees in each corner flying in the directions indicated.

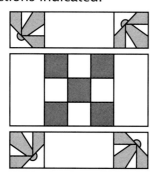

5. Assemble 1 block with large bee center and 3½″ x 6½″ white rectangles. Stitch the small bees in each corner flying in the directions indicated.

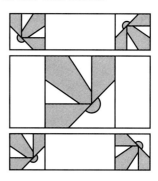

6. Sew 5 horizontal rows alternating 4 blocks with five 1½″ x 12½″ sashing strips. Sew 6 horizontal sashing rows alternating four 1½″ x 12½″ sashing strips and five 1½″ squares.

7. Sew alternating rows of blocks and sashing together using 5 rows of blocks and 6 rows of sashing according to whole quilt diagram.

8. Hand or machine embroider bee antennae.

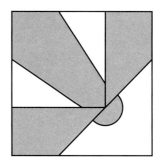

Border

The border for this quilt is sewn in rounds one strip at a time. Alternately add strips to the short sides (top and bottom) and then to the longer sides.

9. For first round of border, sew 2 short strips alternating 4 white Q pieces with 3 purple P pieces. Attach a purple Y piece to each end and sew to top and bottom of quilt. Sew 2 long strips alternating 5 white Q pieces with 6 purple P pieces. Sew to sides of quilt.

10. For second round of border, sew 2 short strips alternating 4 white S pieces with 3 purple R pieces. Attach a purple W piece to each end and sew to top and bottom of quilt. Sew 2 long strips alternating 5 white S pieces with 6 purple R pieces. Sew to sides of quilt.

11. For third round of border, sew 2 short strips alternating 4 white U pieces with 3 purple T pieces. Attach a purple U piece to each end and sew to top and bottom of quilt. Sew 2 long strips alternating 5 white U pieces with 6 purple T pieces. Sew to sides of quilt.

12. For fourth round of border, sew 2 short strips alternating 4 white W pieces with 3 purple V pieces. Attach a purple S piece to each end and sew to top and bottom of quilt. Sew 2 long strips alternating 5 white W pieces with 6 purple V pieces. Sew to sides of quilt.

13. For fifth round of border, sew 2 short strips alternating 4 white Y pieces with 3 purple X pieces. Attach a purple Q piece to each end and sew to top and bottom of quilt. Sew 2 long borders alternating 5 white Y pieces with 6 purple X pieces. Sew to sides of quilt.

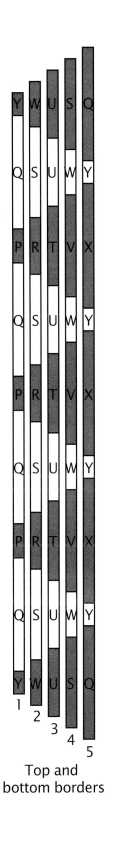

Top and bottom borders

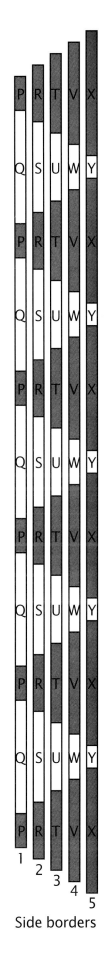

Side borders

85

BEES IN THE FRIENDSHIP GARDEN

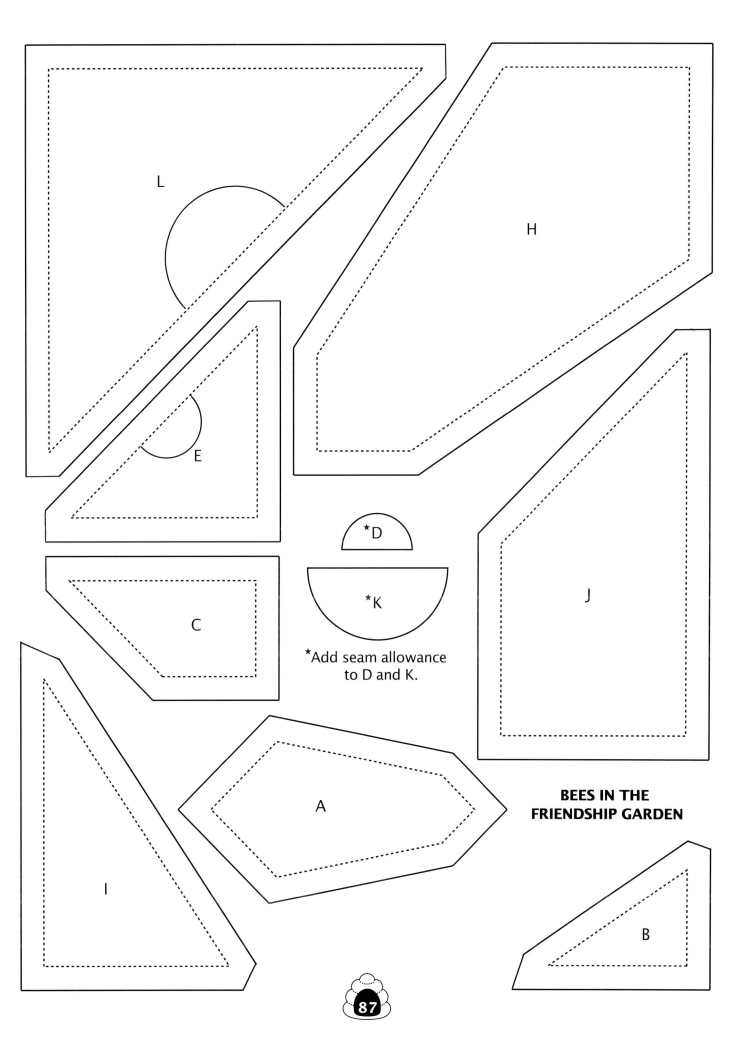

L

H

E

★D

★K

C

J

*Add seam allowance to D and K.

I

A

BEES IN THE FRIENDSHIP GARDEN

B

PROGRESSIVE STRIP QUILT
Designed by Emmy Midkiff

This project is designed to include each member of the bee in the making of a group quilt measuring approximately 65½″ by 91½″. The large task of making a quilt is broken down into a series of small tasks or expenditures listed on the following chart. Each bee member can sign her name indicating which of the 25 tasks she is willing to do. The following instruction sign-up sheet lists the tasks. For a smaller group, each member can sign up for two or three jobs until all are assigned. Even if some members of the group have little time for sewing, they can help in some way. To begin, select the sashing—a solid or a print that appears solid. This will help calm the busy prints in the stripping section. Now choose fabrics for the strips that coordinate with the sashing.

Messages and names of the participants can be written or quilted in the sashing to commemorate the occasion. This pleasing quilt, shown on page 54, resembles a quilter's closet—stacks of colorful fabrics one on top of the other.

This project is well suited for a number of occasions:
- Going away
- Charitable donation
- Baby gift
- Marriage or anniversary celebration
- Healing quilt to make someone feel cherished
- Thank-you for a job well done—volunteer, officer of a group
- Fund-raising project

Progressive Strip Quilt

	DUE DATE	CONTRIBUTION	VOLUNTEER(S)
1	3-1	Furnish 1⅔ yds. solid fabric for sashing strips and borders. Wash & iron. Cut 8 strips of sashing 2½″ x 42½″ and give to 2nd set of "strippers". Cut 8 strips 4″ x 42½″ for border. Give to _____.	#1
2	3-15	Make two 10½″ wide x 42½″ long sections from a variety of scrap fabrics. Cut strips 1½″ to 4″ wide by 10½″ long. Give to _____. Make eight 10½″ wide x 42½″ long sections from a variety of scrap fabrics. Cut strips 1½″ to 4″ wide by 10½″ long. Sew long strip of sashing to left side of each. Give to _____.	#2-11
3	4-5	Assemble quilt top. Give to _____.	#12
4	4-5	Furnish 4⅔ yds. fabric for backing. Wash & iron. Cut 2 pieces 42½″ x 70″. From remaining fabric cut two 12″ x 35¼″ pieces; stitch end to end and use for center panel. Backing should measure 70″ x 96″. Give to _____.	#13
5	4-5	Furnish 81″ x 96″ bonded polyester batt. Give to _____.	#14
6	4-5	Collect donations for the $_____ needed to pay for machine quilting ($_____ each). Give to _____.	#15-21
7	5-3	Arrange for and take quilt to _____ for machine quilting. Pick quilting pattern. Pick up quilt when finished. Give to _____.	#22
8	5-3	Furnish ¾ yd. fabric for binding. Wash & iron. Cut 8 strips 3″ wide x 42″ long. Fold in half lengthwise and iron. Give to _____.	#23
9	5-17	Bind quilt and sew a label on the back. Give to _____.	#24
10	5-17	Take photographs of quilt. Take quilt to shelter.	#25

2. 42½″ ← → 10½″

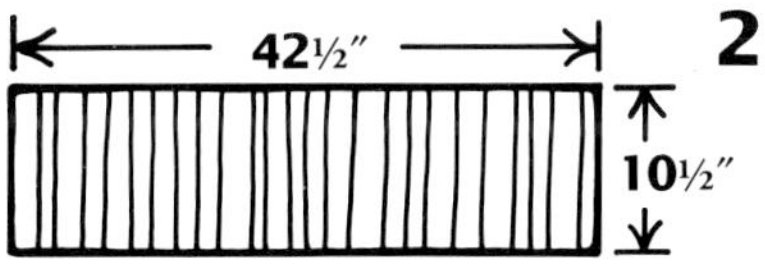

2. SASHING 42½″ ← → 10½″

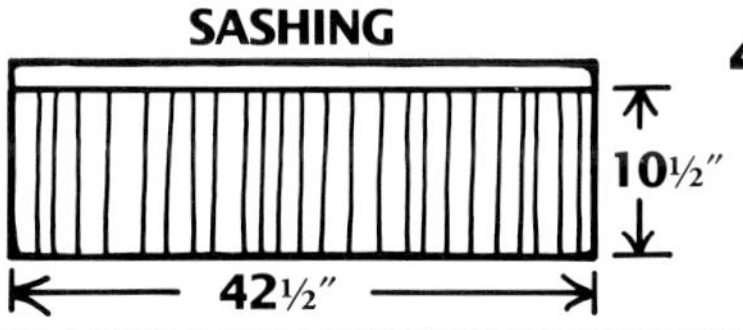

4. 96″ 70″ A B A B

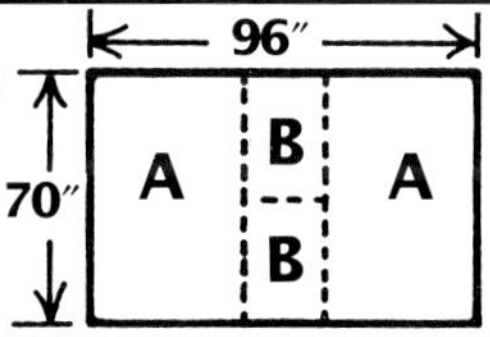

A. 42½″ x 70″
B. 12″ x 35¼″

PROGRESSIVE STRIP QUILT
Designed by Emmy Midkiff

Finished Size 65½" x 91½"

Before assembly, strip pieced units are 10½" x 42½".
Measurements given on quilt are cut measurements.
Seam allowance is ¼".

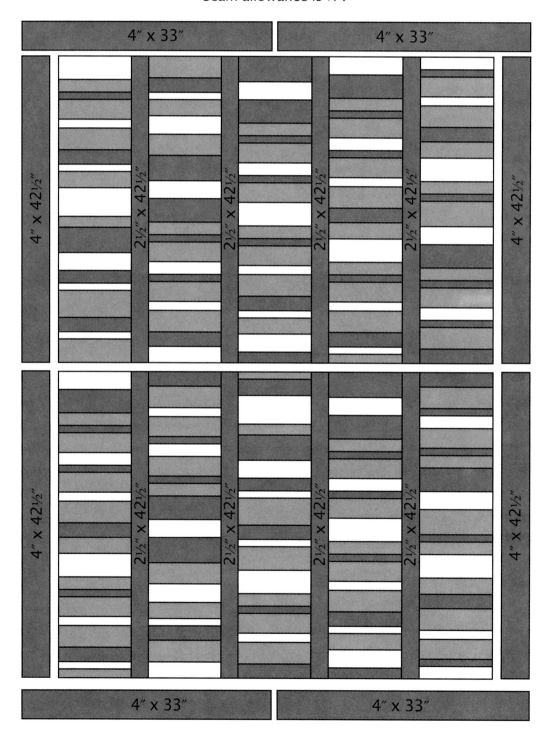

AUTOGRAPH BLOCK

Finished Block Size 6″

For each block, cut:
2 A print
1 B background

Piece as illustrated.

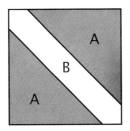

Zig-Zag

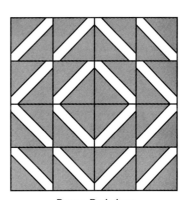

Barn Raising

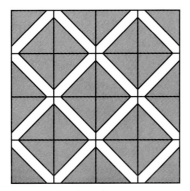

Lattice

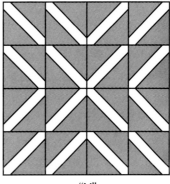

"X"

HIDDEN HEARTS
Designed by Barbara Lister

Finished Block Size 8″

For each block, cut:
2 A print
1 B background
1 C, 1 Cr print
2 D background
1 E background

Piece as illustrated.

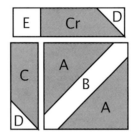

Possible Sets

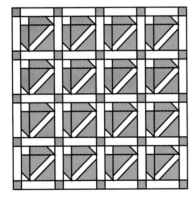

Set with sashing

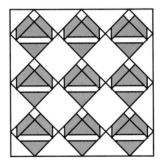

With setting blocks

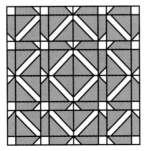

Barn Raising

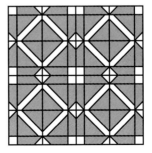

Lattice

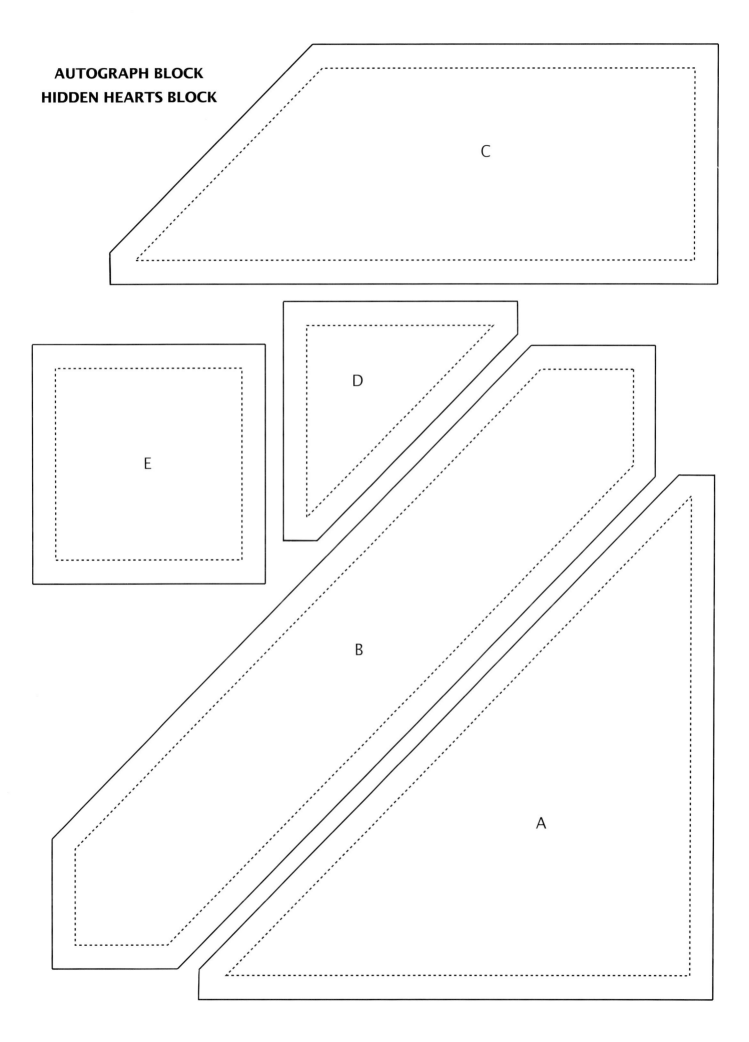

AUTOGRAPH BLOCK
HIDDEN HEARTS BLOCK

C

D

E

B

A

CAFFEINE DELIGHT

Designed by Sherri Driver

Finished Block Size 18″ x 6″

Cup, saucer and handle for one coffee cup
can be cut from a 7″ x 7″ square of fabric.

For each block, cut:
3 A print
1 B, 1 Br background
2 C background
3 D print
6 E background
1 background strip 1¾″ x 18½″
1 tablecloth print strip 1¾″ x 18½″

For each cup handle, cut bias strip 1″ x 5″,
fold in half lengthwise twice. Before
piecing block, appliqué handles to
background pieces as illustrated.

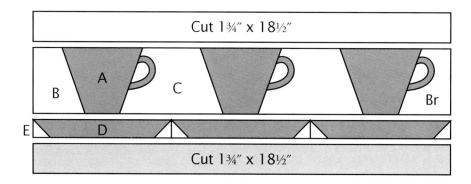

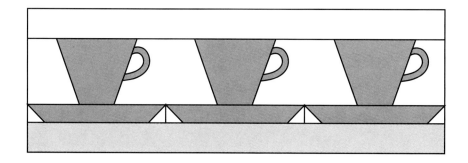

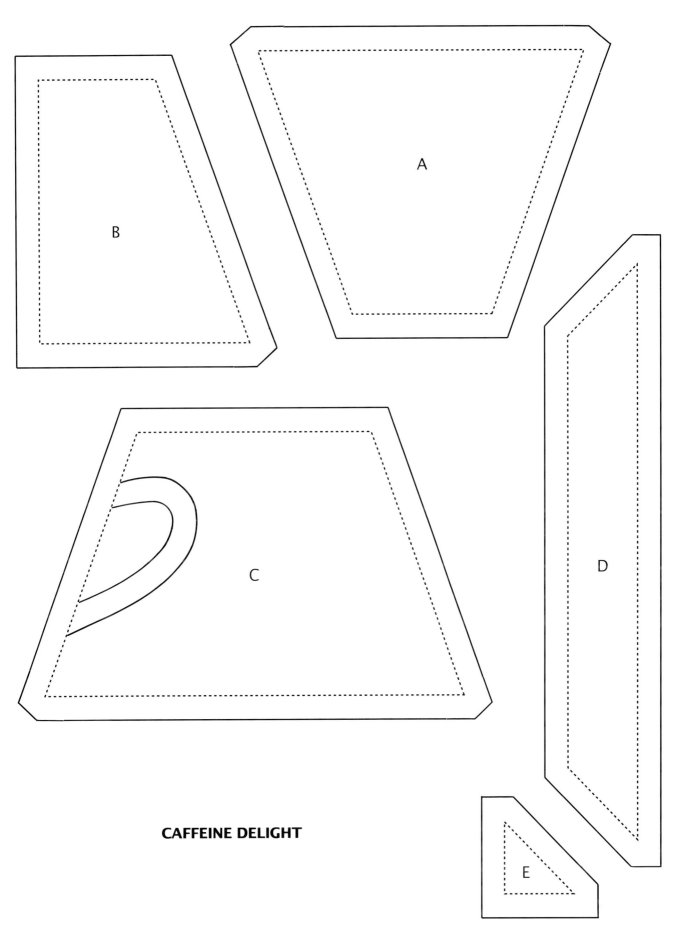

CAFFEINE DELIGHT

CENTENNIAL TREES
Designed by Judy Kraus

Finished Block Size 15″ x 9″

Cut for one block:
star – 4 B, 1 D
tree #1 – 1 E, 1 H, 1 K
tree #2 – 1 E, 1 H, 1 L, 1Lr
tree #3 – 1 E, 1 H, 1 F
tree #4 – 1 E, 1 H, 1 F
background – 2 A, 1 Ar, 4 B, 1 C (no pattern
    piece given - cut C 2″ x 12½″), 1 D, 2 E,
    2 F, 1 G, 1 H, 1 I, 2 Ir, 1 J, 1 M

Assemble strips following diagram. Sew
strips together.

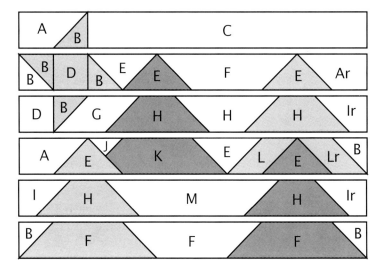

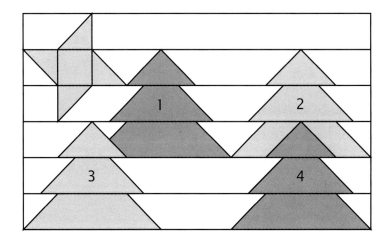

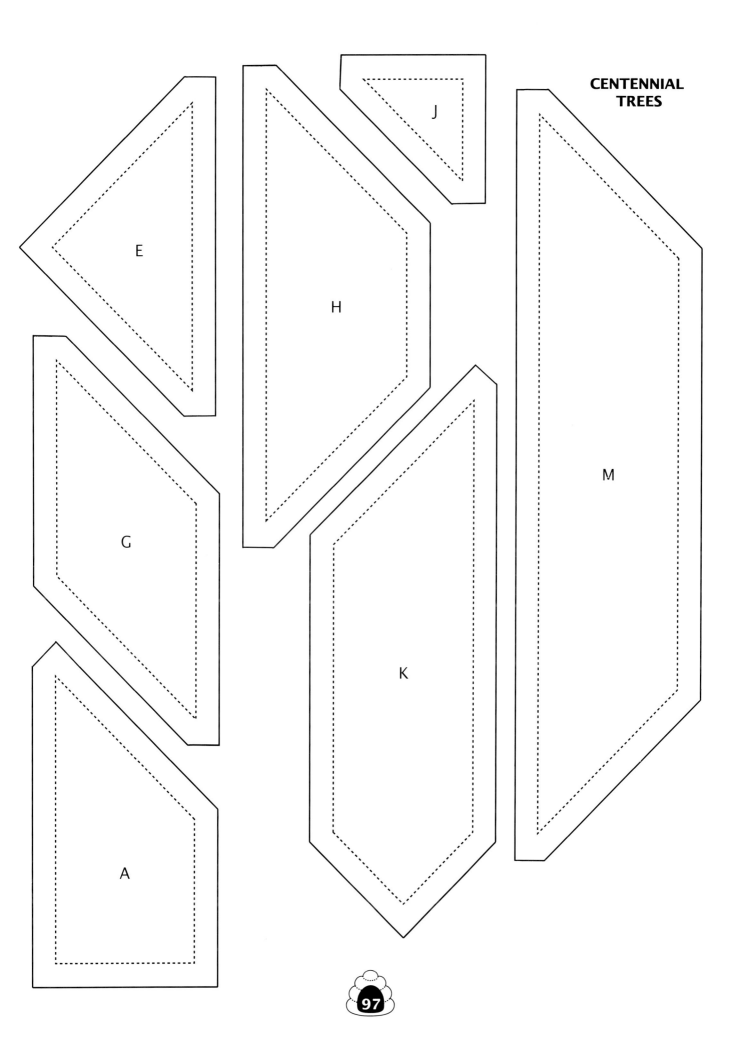

E

H

J

CENTENNIAL
TREES

G

M

A

K

97

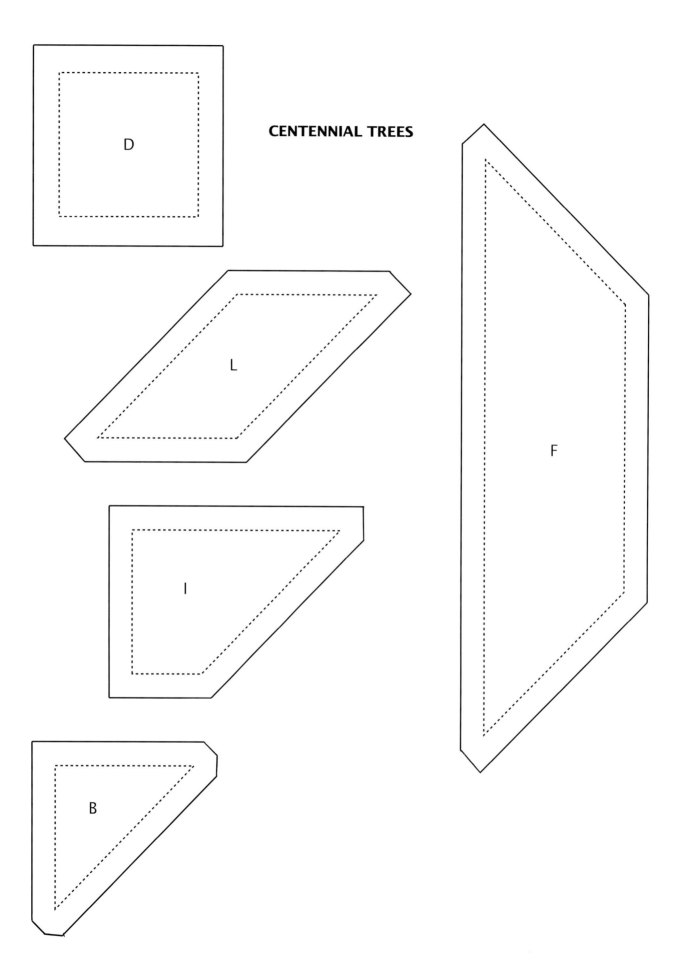

CENTENNIAL TREES

D

L

I

F

B

MOUNTAIN MAJESTY
Designed by Mary (Sandy) Sanford

Finished Block Size 18″ x 6″

Cut for one block:
dark – 1 A, 2 E, 1 G
medium – 1 B, 2 C
background – 1 D, 1 Dr, 2 C, 2 F

Piece block following diagram. Appliqué
sun or moon as shown.

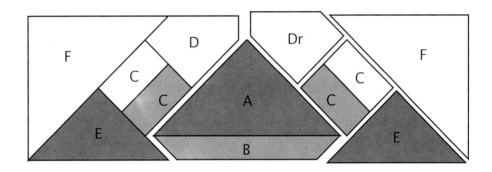

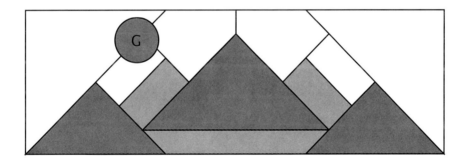

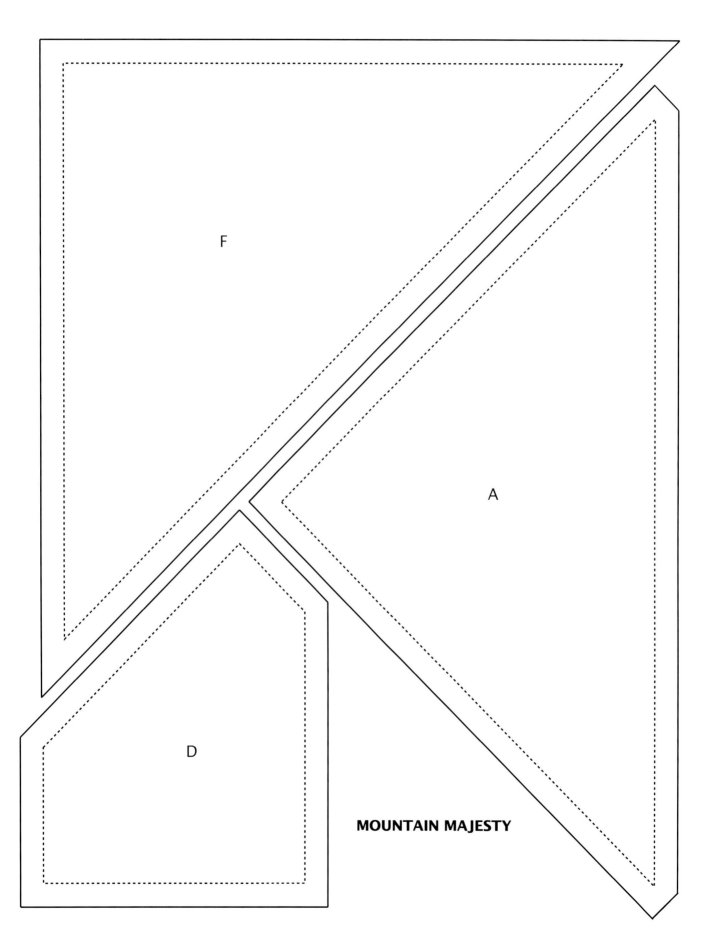

F

A

D

MOUNTAIN MAJESTY

100

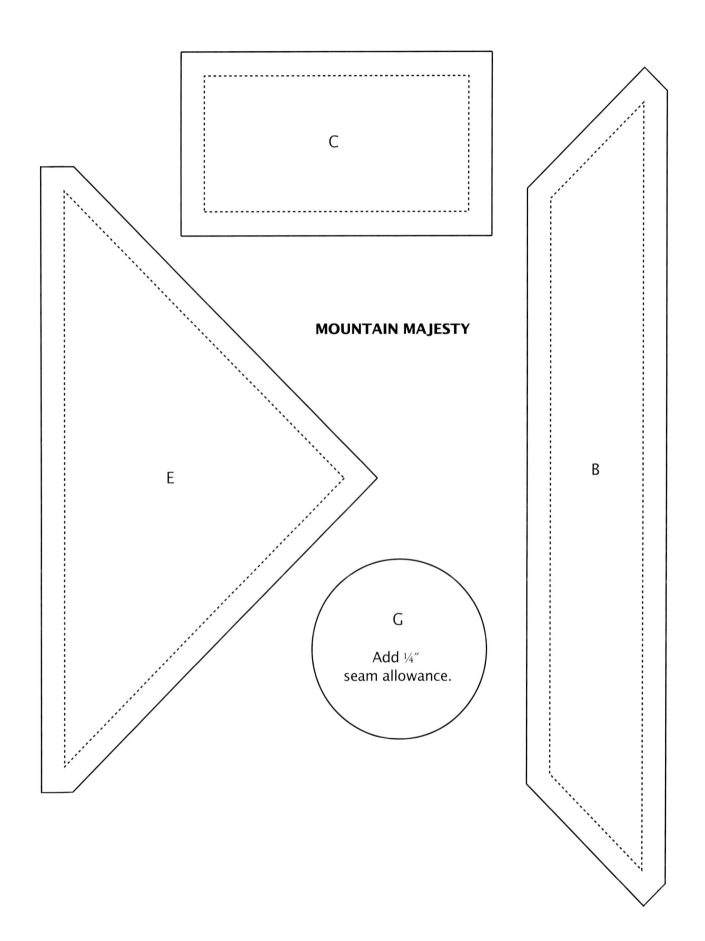

C

MOUNTAIN MAJESTY

E

B

G

Add ¼″
seam allowance.

THE KEYBOARD
Designed by Mary Beth Church

Finished Block Size 12″ x 6″

Cut 12½″ x 6½″ rectangle. Machine satin stitch outlines of white keys at 1″ intervals. Appliqué dark keys (¾″ x 4″ finished) following diagram. Cut one hand and one hand reversed; appliqué in place using photos on pages 40 and 41 as a guide.

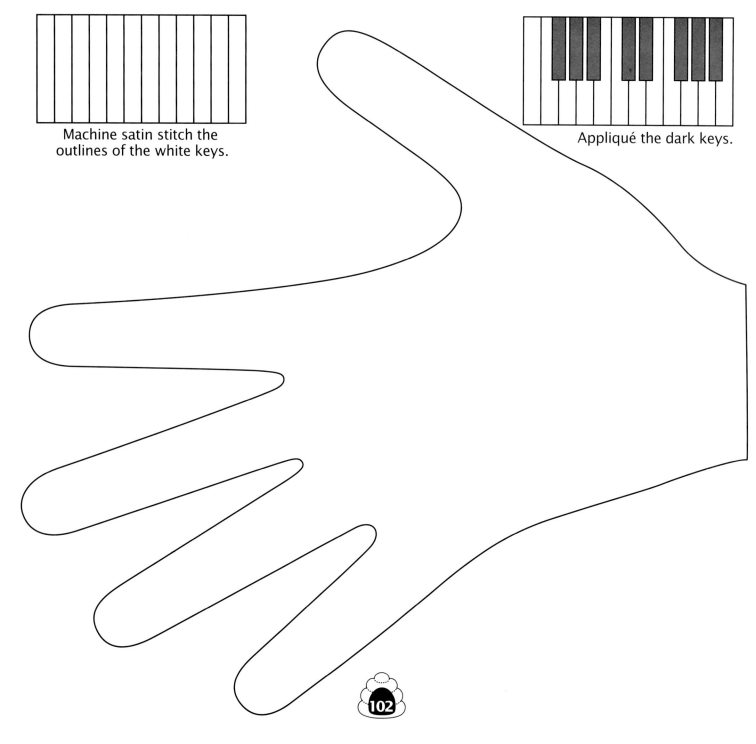

Machine satin stitch the outlines of the white keys.

Appliqué the dark keys.

▼ RESOURCES ▼

ABC Quilts, Sherburne Hill Rd., Northwood, Hew Hampshire, 03261 – (603) 942-7778
Quilters Hall of Fame, P.O. Box 681, Marion, Ohio 46952
Ronald McDonald's House, One McDonald's Plaza, Oakbrook, Illinois 60521, or consult
    the local Yellow Pages under McDonald's, Ronald House
Scrap Soup Pasta: Great American Quilt Factory, Inc., 8970 E. Hampden Ave., Denver,
    Colorado 80231 USA

Computer Services:
CompuServe – 1-800-848-8199
GEnie Information Services – 1-800-638-9636
National Video Tex Network (NVN) – 1-800-336-9092
Prodigy – 1-800-284-5933

Hoffman Challenge:
Betty Boyink, 818 Sheldon Rd., Grand Haven, Michigan 49417
Holice Turnbow, 2029 Ashley Dr., Shepherdstown, West Virginia 25443

▼ BIBLIOGRAPHY ▼

A Guide to Pink Elephants. Richards Rosen Associates, Inc., New York, 1952.
Ahlberg, Janet and Allan. *Each Peach, Pear, Plum.* Penguin Books Ltd., Harmondsworth, Middlesex,
    England, 1978.
Better Homes and Gardens Kids' Snacks. Meredith Corporations, Des Moines, Iowa, 1986.
Betty Crocker's Picture Cook Book. McGraw-Hill Book Company, Inc. and General Mills, Inc., 1950.
Boyink, Betty. *Nautical Voyages for Quilters.* Betty Boyink Publishing, Grand Haven, Michigan, 1990.
Carter, Christal. *Holiday Happenings.* That Patchwork Place, Inc., Bothell, Washington, 1987.
Clark, Cindy Taylor. Old St. Nick and Antique Toys. Cindy Taylor Clark Designs, Alfred, Maine, 1983.
Cooper, Patricia, and Norma Bradley Buferd. *The Quilters, Women and Domestic Art.* Doubleday & Co.,
    Inc., Garden City, New York, 1977.
Gardner, Shirley. The Evergreen Quilt. Shirley Gardner Designs, Evergreen, Colorado, 1989.
Holland, Anna. Rainbow Over My Zoo. Waterford, Virginia, 1988.
Kansas History, Vol. 13, Spring 1990, No. 1. Kansas State Historical Society, Topeka, Kansas, 1990.
Martin, Judy. *Scrap Quilts.* Moon Over the Mountain Publishing, Wheat Ridge, Colorado, 1985.
Martin, Judy. *Scraps, Blocks & Quilts.* Crosley-Griffith Publishing, Denver, 1990.
Martin, Judy. *Judy Martin's Ultimate Book of Quilt Block Patterns.* Crosley-Griffith Publishing, Denver, 1988.
Miller, Pat; Edie Acsell, and Antoinette Sforza. *Crimes of Passion in the Kitchen.* Cookery & Co.,
    Englewood, Colorado, 1982.
Nadelstern, Paula and Lyn Nell Hancock. *Quilting Together.* Crown Publishing, Inc., New York, 1988.
Random House Webster's College Dictionary. Random House, Inc., New York, 1991.
Smith, Nancy, and Lynda Milligan. *Always Angels.* Possibilities, Denver, 1991.
Snowbound. Red Wagon, Liberty, Missouri, 1989.
Steinem, Gloria. Interview. Oprah Winfrey Show, January 19, 1993.
Variable Star Quilters. *The Quiltie Ladies Scrapbook.* Indian Valley Printing Ltd., Souderton,
    Pennsylvania, 1987.
Wilkes, Angela. *My First Cook Book.* Alfred A. Knopf, New York, 1989.

Other Publications from Possibilities
CREATIVITY FOR ALL AGES!

SEWING MACHINE FUN
Fun projects to build sewing machine artistry and skills. Self-directed skill-building activities for kids 7 and up.
DS1–72 pages–$15.95

MORE SEWING MACHINE FUN
More projects to build sewing machine artistry and skills. Self-directed skill-building activities for kids 7 and up.
DS2–72 pages–$15.95

**T.L.C.
TENDER LOVING COVERS**
Captivating pictorial quilts for children and decorating, made with an easy triangle method called Fast Forty-Fives.
POS-15–136 pages–$19.95

COTTONWOOD PASS
Barbara Barr has designed eight inspirational pieced floral blocks that can be used in a variety of combinations. Plus five pretty pillow patterns.
POS-16–40 pages–$12.95

DECK THE HALLS
Quilts, wallhangings, pillows, fabric holly wreath, KIDS' PROJECTS, garland, stockings, tree skirt, everything the family needs for Christmas fun!
POS-1–64 pages–$15.95

P.S. I LOVE YOU
One of the top 10 quilting books in America. 17 quilts in cradle, crib and twin. Bumper pads, dust ruffle, accessories. Exceptional collection!
POS-3–80 pages–$16.95

QUILTS SEW QUICK
Terrific for beginning quilters, quick gifts, or fast, utility quilts. 7 quilts in 3 sizes each. Large patches for today's large print fabrics.
POS-12–28 pages–$9.95

SISTERS & QUILTS
Celebration of quilts and sisterhood by award-winning quilters. 17 original quilt designs span lives of sisters, birth to "fancy free" years.
POS-13–112 pages–$19.95

ALWAYS ANGELS
Over 20 easy-to-make creative holiday projects featuring angels. Quilt, tree skirt, sweatshirt, wreath, wrapping paper, gift bag, placemats, and more!
POS-6–24 pages–$8.95

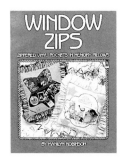

BUNCHIES
Ideas & instructions for an assortment of fast & easy Bunchies hair ornaments. Shag, flash net, sew-free, basic, fancy seams, bitsy, & others.
POS-14–24 pages–$7.95

WINDOW ZIPS
Unique memorabilia pillows with zippered vinyl pockets. Designs for baby, a family trip, a special school year, sports stars, quilters, & moving away.
POS-10–28 pages–$8.95

HOLIDAY WINDOWS
More memorabilia designs for zippered vinyl pocket pillows. Christmas, birthday, Valentine's Day, Easter, Halloween, snowman.
POS-11–28 pages–$8.95

MEMORY QUILTS
Over 15 innovative designs & ideas for planning one-of-a-kind memory quilts. Explores photos on fabric...the '90s version of memory quilts.
POS-8–104 pages–$19.95

YESTERDAY'S CHARM
Hand or contemporary applique methods let you capture both the beauty & the spirit of quiltmaking. Ten floral blocks, 4 different versions.
POS-9–20 pages–$8.95

Check with your local quilt shop.
If not available, write or call us directly.

8970 E. Hampden Ave., Denver CO 80231   303-740-6206   FAX 303-220-7424   Order # 1-800-474-2665